If you enjoy reading about Norfolk and Suffolk, Cambridgeshire and Essex, look for titles from 'Poppyland Publishing'.

Available at the time of printing:

The 'East Anglian Memories' series
  Those Seaside Days

The 'Albums' series
  The Rows of Yarmouth
  A Mundesley Album
  A Cromer Album
  A Sheringham Album
  Sheringham – A Century of Change

The 'Norfolk Origins' series
  Hunters to First Farmers
  Roads and Tracks
  Celtic Fire and Roman Rule

Local History Booklets
  Great Yarmouth – History, Herring and Holidays
  Fakenham – Town on the Wensum
  Coltishall – Heyday of a Broadland Village
  Caister – 2000 Years a Village
  Have You Heard about Blakeney?
  The Cromer Lifeboats
  Weybourne – Peaceful Mirror of a Turbulent Past
  Salthouse – Village of Character and History
  Cley – Living with Memories of Greatness
  Poppyland – Strands of Norfolk History
  The Hunstanton Lifeboats
  Palling – A History Shaped by the Sea
  Caister – Beach Boats and Beachmen

Miscellaneous Titles
  Taking the Children Too...
  The Birds of Sheringham
  East Anglia on Film
  His Majesty's Late Ship the Invincible

Many more titles are in preparation. For a current list, ask at your bookshop or write to Poppyland Publishing, 13, Kings Arms Street, North Walsham, Norfolk NR28 9JX

Other titles in this series:

'Those Seaside Days' by Jean Grose. Recollections of seaside holidays in Norfolk in the 1940s.

WHEN WHERRIES SAILED BY

RECOLLECTIONS OF A BROADLAND VILLAGE

Olga Sinclair

The 'East Anglian Memories' series

The Artist

In 1930 Joan Young came with her parents, Jack and May Gibling, to live at Rosemary Cottage in St James, Coltishall. The cottage, over 200 years old, was formerly occupied by three generations of the Thrower family, blacksmiths. Their 'shop' (smithy) stood opposite the cottage.

After leaving school she studied drawing at Norwich Art School then worked in commercial art. After a few years in Norwich she returned with husband Derek and three children to live in St James, where their own house was built on the Walnut Meadow.

Joan Young has latterly studied watercolour and has had several successful exhibitions over the last ten years. Coltishall is still her home and nearly 60 years on she remembers with affection many of the people and their activities which form the subject of this book.

© Olga Sinclair and Poppyland Publishing 1987
First published 1987
ISBN: 0 946148 27 9

Printed and bound by Speedprint Design, Spalding, Lincolnshire.
Illustrations and cover by Joan Young.

Contents

Introduction

I moved to Coltishall with my husband and three small sons in 1954. Our house, The Beeches, had been built in about 1841 and our garden of over three acres included a disused marlpit with an old brick kiln adjoining. How fortunate we were to have so much space, to have outbuildings which included an old barn, ideal for folk-dancing and parties, above which was a loft for the boys' club-room and museum.

In the 23 happy years we lived there I developed an intense love for the village, being fascinated not only by how it was then, but also by hearing of how it had been in the past. I am very grateful to all those who talked to me, in many instances allowing me to tape record their recollections. These, together with some items from documentary research, going back even further, I now have pleasure in sharing with anyone who cares to read them. Part of the proceeds of the sale of the book will go to Coltishall Parish Council towards an amenity in the village.

In particular I would like to thank Mrs E Beevor, Walter Coman, Bert Digby, Peter Francis, Gordon Jarvis, Rev Lee, Billy Stibbons, Walter Watts and Audrey Wilson.

I also remember with gratitude those who are no longer with us – Mr Billy Allen, John Coman, George Humm, Beth Paterson, Ralph and Mary Wells and Willie Wilson. My thanks also to The Norwich Record Office for permission to use extracts from the Dorothy Kingsbury volume (ref: MC29 468X).

O.S. August 1987

When Wherries Sailed

As many as twenty wherries would 'drop down' on Coltishall on a single tide, so the old watermen recall - and what a marvellous sight that must have been! Imagine their majestic approach, a convoy of huge black sails, silent save for the ripple of the water, the singing of the wind in the rigging, the creak of boards and the occasional shouts of the wherrymen. They came from Great Yarmouth, a distance of twenty miles or more, carrying coal mostly, brought from the pits of the north of Britain and shipped direct from the colliers into the wherries which tied up alongside. That way they avoided landing charges.

They had shot under Wroxham Bridge, lowering their masts at the last possible moment so that their way carried them clear of the low archway. Then up again would go the huge mast, the sails were rapidly unfurled and on they would proceed with scarcely a check in their progress, along the winding reaches, past Belaugh church on its high promontory, conspicuous for many miles, the river seeming loathe to leave it. The channel leading to the disused chalk and lime workings, known as Little Switzerland, was already closed and private, but that was not their destination.

A view from Coltishall bridge, looking towards Hautbois House, with a wherry in the foreground. (Photo: Norwich City Library)

Ladies in the grounds of Coltishall Hall, believed to be the Squire's wife, Mrs Rogers, and a companion. (Photo: Audrey Wilson)

They sailed into Coltishall, past the lower common, an area of rough grass, often today called Coltishall Green. It rolled from road to river populated, not by holiday-makers as now, but by geese and goats and donkeys. On the opposite bank lay marshes, water meadows where cattle grazed in summer, winter home of a flock of wild geese, stretching in beauty and peace to the distant woods of Heggatt.

The river sweeps away almost at right angles by the Rising Sun Inn, then twists back sharply out of sight along Manor House Reach, towards the mill and the lock. Some wherries tied up at the end of the common, at the Rising Sun wharf, others carried on further upstream to a staithe at the end of Mead Loke or passed through the lock to the staithe by the bridge at the White Horse. A few went further still to Bream Corner, whence coal could be carted to the lime kilns at Great Hautbois. Some went beyond the village and on to Oxnead, Buxton or Aylsham.

Coltishall has several large and pleasant houses, many of which were built during the eighteenth and nineteenth centuries, for it has long had something of a cachet as a fashionable place to live. In past centuries it had excellent facilities both for shopping and as a centre of commerce and was able to supply just about everything its inhabitants, rich or poor, might need. It was a place of sturdy self-sufficiency, where most of the men and women were employed within the village, particularly on farms, in maltings, boatyards and lime-pits. Earlier there had been work in brewing too.

The wherries brought in a huge amount of coal, the bulk of which was used in the maltings, but large quantities were also consumed in the grates of the village houses, for solid fuel was the only means of heating and cooking. The merchant at the Rising Sun delivered it in his horsedrawn cart and if the price charged had risen to £1 per ton there were groans about hard times. In the big houses fires were lit in almost every room in the winter, and everywhere lighting depended on paraffin and candles.

Life Was Tougher Then

 In Lion Road there was a butcher's shop owned by Mrs Crowe; it was built of wood and attached to the end wall of her house. Behind the shop were sheds where animals were stalled in readiness for slaughter and the slaughter-house itself was situated nearby.

"I remember well when sent on an errand to the butcher's shop on one occasion seeing on my arrival the slaughter of a bullock," Mr Allen related in his reminiscences. "There was the animal with its head held down by a rope passed through a ring firmly fixed in the floor and a man struck it with a pole-axe in the middle of the forehead. Death appeared to be instantaneous but one cannot help wondering what it would have meant if the blow had not been accurate. It was spectacular but far from humane. In those days the humane killer, if known, was seldom used."

Next door to the King's Head was a General Store. It kept groceries of all kinds and also food for pigs and poultry, sweets and minor articles of wearing apparel. Over the door was a notice that the proprietor, Mrs Allen was licensed to sell tobacco and cigarettes, both were sold by weight and cost about 3½d an ounce. This shop also sold pork.

It was a common thing for a cottager to buy a young pig and get credit for the supply of food from the store-keeper until such time as the pig was ready for slaughter. Some of the meat and offal was kept for the family's own use and the store-keeper paid for the rest of the carcase, after deducting the amount owing for its food. Generally this amounted to enough to pay at least one quarter's rent for the cottager. Billy Allen recalled being with the landlord of one of these cottages and hearing the tenant say he could not pay the rent till the next week as the pig was not being killed till then. The landlord was quite satisfied.

The allotments in those days were full of pigs, there was a sty on almost every plot and the pig feed was supplemented by pieces from the house, potato peelings and scraps. It was usually the rent for the Michaelmas quarter that was paid in this way, for in those days pork was considered out of season during the summer. As a treat young Billy Allen was sometimes allowed to turn the handle of the sausage machine. Apart from the addition of a few breadcrumbs the sausages were truly pork and the pork cheeses, or brawns they made were one of his special delights.

That shop was the only one in that part of the village, for where the newspaper and stationer's shop now stands were two houses and there were seven other small houses down the yard alongside it. In those nine houses lived about fifty men, women and children. One house had only one living-room, one bedroom and a lean-to, like an attic with a single glass tile in the roof to let in a little light, yet in that primitive accommodation a family of eight children was brought up. Families of seven or eight children were quite common in those days.

They had a shared privy which was a hut with a seat over a deep hole. It was emptied out once or twice a year, from the back - and that was a day to keep out of the vicinity if possible - 'it reeked to high heaven!' There was one pump in the yard and the well from which they drew their water was shared by the people at The Limes, who also had a pump on their side of their garden wall.

There were no gardens attached to those houses but most of the tenants had allotments and kept a pig or maybe a few chickens which would mostly be fed on scraps, anything that could be spared from the house. Those houses were demolished when the council houses were built in Rectory Road in 1936/37, just before the Second World War. Only the end cottage was left because preparations were being made for air raid precautions and it was decided they could use that as a mortuary in the event of a disastrous air-raid. Fortunately it was never put to that macabre use.

Next to those slums stood The Limes, which Pevsner calls 'the finest house in the village'. It has a forecourt flanked by outbuildings with stabling for eight horses which had been built on about a hundred years after the house. It has a facade of mellow red brick with seven bays, a recessed centre, a hipped roof and a fine doorway with Doric pilasters and a segmental pediment. The house carries the date 1692 and towards the end of the eighteenth century it was the home of Mary Hardy who kept a diary recording much day to day information about her life there. Allowing the house to justify its name is not easy in these days - at the beginning of the century there were two fine lime trees at the edge of the path outside its wall which were lopped every few years, but in time they had to be removed for road widening and the new trees planted to replace them have difficulty in surviving with the pressure of today's traffic and have been knocked into more than once.

In the days of the wherries, the road to the church, known as 'the hill' was narrow, dusty, surfaced with flint and gravel, sunk deep between high banks with hedges on either side. It led through a short stretch of undeveloped fields where trees hid the church from view. Along this road on Sunday it was a familiar sight to see the Squire, his wife and all their servants marching to morning service, two by two, almost like a regiment. The staff alone filled about three rows of pews, and among them was a page boy in a tight-fitting jacket ornamented by a double row of shining brass buttons - dozens of buttons all the way up the front - and a pillbox hat. Every member of the staff, indoor and out, had to go to church - being in service was nearly like being in the army then.

The Bloater King

Opposite the church was another general store and this one also doubled as a pork butchers - pork for some reason was always considered different from 'butcher's meat'. Close by was the first of the two fishmongers in the village. Robert Pike had a smoke-house at the top of Chapel Lane and in about 1906 Ralph Wells, then about nine years old, got himself a job with this fishmonger. He 'lugged' a basket of bloaters around the houses in Church Street and up Rectory Road, knocking on the doors and selling them. The herrings came in tubs from Great Yarmouth to Coltishall Station and 'old Bob Pike' picked them up there in his pony and cart; the cart was brightly painted and carried the proud designation '*R. K. Pike - the Bloater King*' on the back.

The herrings were washed and threaded by the gills on to sticks - *speets* they called them - and put in the smoke house. It was a shed built of thick wooden sleepers, with a good roof. Robert Pike would climb up a ladder and hang the *speets* festooned with herrings just below the roof. Then the fire was lit below, burning oak wood and plenty of saw-dust to keep it damped down and make it smoke. It made a lovely smell - Ralph's mouth watered as he remembered it. 'Never was any bloaters like them!'

Once a week, in the morning before school, Ralph set out with fifty bloaters in his basket. They were a penny each. He soon came to know the houses where people were likely to buy from him - some folks he felt were a bit too snooty to want bloaters, so he didn't go to them, but many others were glad to get a nourishing, cheap meal. If Ralph sold out the fishmonger gave him fourpence, but if he had some left he only got threepence. He started out at 7 o'clock and had to hurry to get round in time to have breakfast and go to school.

On Down The Street

A little further along was Libby Wright's shop where the children bought their sweets on the way to or from school. Every afternoon when he came out of infant's school, little Billy Stibbons went to visit his great aunt and uncle, who lived close by in Kimberley Terrace. They gave him a piece of cake, a glass of water and a farthing. His sisters had the same. They were always instructed not to spend the money, to take it home and put it in their money boxes, but they used to run back to Libby Wright's and get liquorice - yards of it for a farthing. It used to hang on a peg like bootlaces, or you could get a lucky bag. 'That was where all my farthings went, I don't think I ever took one home to put in my money box. I always went straight out and spent it.'

Opposite the church was Libby Wright's shop, where the children bought their sweets. (Photo: Norwich City Library)

Billy Allen also associated this shop with liquorice chains and pear drops. 'I seldom if ever, ate a liquorice chain after I left the village school, then fifty years later, when evacuated to Wales' (by which time he was himself a teacher) 'I passed a small sweet shop out of which walked two of my pupils with liquorice chains. They offered me a share and immediately I went back in memory and was again a schoolboy trudging home from school.'

Some of the young customers used to tease the kindly old lady who kept the shop. When three or four boys each had a farthing to spend, they would not all go in together, but separately, at sufficient intervals for her to get

In the garden of the Limes. Mr and Mrs Stibbons with their children Hilda, Billy and Mabel. The basket tables and chairs were made in the village at Thixtons. (Photo: Audrey Wilson)

back to her sitting-room behind the shop. As soon as she was away the next one would open the door, making the bell jangle loudly to summon her back. But the joke fell flat, for the lady refused to get annoyed - she understood children and knew that to ignore their teasing was the surest way of depriving them of the fun they expected.

Farthings often came into the prices of those days, particularly for items of clothing. There was a shop selling ladies' wear, kept by a widow and her daughter who could supply almost any article of feminine frippery from stays to Sunday hats and their prices had a tendency to be as inconvenient as possible with regard to the giving of change. The odd farthing frequently came into the price and then the purchaser would be asked to accept a packet of pins in lieu of the farthing.

On the island site, now occupied by the garage and petrol pumps stood the premises of Walter Vout, master carpenter. Hedges and fences tight to the road enclosed his woodyard and often there was a huge tree trunk resting on the saw-pit in the process of being planked, of which more will be said later.

The top common stretched towards the lock and beyond that was one of the loveliest industrial buildings in Norfolk - the high, white, weather-boarded water mill. The horses of the local traders grazed on the common, ancient lime trees bordered the grass and almost always there were lines of linen strung from post to post, flapping in the breeze. A sudden shower would send the housewives scurrying across to fetch in the washing, but in fine weather it was a pleasant place to linger for a gossip.

There were two carriers plying to Norwich three or four days a week. George Marsh went to the Wagon and Horses on Tombland on Mondays,

Horstead Mill, one of the loveliest industrial buildings in Norfolk. Whoever hired the bakery had to buy all their flour from the mill.

Wednesdays and Saturdays, departing from Coltishall at 9 a.m. Harry Jeffries, who stabled his horses near the Red Lion, set off on the same days and at the same time for the Duke's Palace in Duke Street. Both, states the Directory 'return on the same day' though presumably at no fixed time. Other transport, gigs and dog-carts, could be hired from various job-masters, and when the football team had an away match, travelling sometimes as far as Mundesley, some twelve miles away, they hired a wagonette from the harness-maker.

The harness-maker's shop has long since been pulled down and with it the stables at the back. Built of red brick, its upper walls mantled thickly with ivy, it stood forward of the White Horse Inn. The shop window, right-angled on the front corner, was glazed with small rectangular panes of glass through which you could look and see the sadddler at work, surrounded by the tools of his trade as well as by a miscellany of saddles, bridles, horse-collars, straps, bags and leather goods of all descriptions.

You could not actually look into the dress-maker's shop to see the girls at work there, but you sometimes saw these young ladies setting out to walk to Wroxham Hall, for the owner was proud to make such fine clothes that she was patronised by the 'gentry'. Her girls reflected this feeling; they preferred

There were two carriers plying to Norwich three days a week. This is George Marsh with his wife.

When the football team played an away match they hired a wagonette. The curate, Rev Goodwin, is standing on the right. Charlie Wells, front right, was killed in the First World War. (Photo: Gordon Jarvis)

to learn the dress-making trade to their alternative of going into service, convinced it was a bit more classy.

It was a long walk to Wroxham Hall, taking at least an hour, starting along the footpath beside the river, where the young ladies studiously ignored the jocular comments of the men on the wherries. From the mill they continued through Heggatt up the hill and along the bridlepath, over high and low bridges, beneath which the old marl diggings had cut such deep ravines the area became known as Little Switzerland. On they went, over the meadows and through the woods till they reached the hall, carrying between them the large basket with partly made or finished garments - dresses fashionably bustled, tight-nipped at the waist, coats or capes long, full-skirted, and lace-frilled underwear. A lovely walk on a fine day, but of course it was not always so.

Bonds Harnessmaker's - you could look through the window and see the saddler at work.

That basket the girls carried was made almost next door to the dress-maker's shop, for there were the premises of the thatcher and basket-maker. Stacks of reeds stood in his yard, brought up by wherry from the reed beds beside the Broads to the north of the village. The osiers were grown locally too, and before they were ready for use they were soaked in the dyke close to the river at the end of the basket-maker's yard.

Across the street was Uriah Earl's, the blacksmith's. His fires would glow bright till eight or nine in the evening and the ring of his hammer could be heard across the village. There was a second smithy in St James, an outlying part of the village and neither stood under a spreading chestnut-tree, but the blacksmiths certainly had brawny arms - and needed them.

This was the heyday of horses and horse-drawn vehicles and rough roads.

The horses had to be shod with iron shoes and the wooden wheels with iron rims. What child could pass by operations of so much interest without lingering? Outside school hours there was bound to be one onlooker or more, watching as the red hot shoe was taken from the furnace, pounded into shape on the anvil, plunged into a tank of water and placed, still hot, to the horse's hoof. Probably there was more pain taken to ensure that that shoe fitted the hoof than was taken in many cases to see that a child's shoe was the right size.

Shoeing a wheel was perhaps even more spectacular. Close to the forge was a large metal wheelplate, which had a hole in the centre with a metal lug, rather like a huge staple. To this the smith attached a perpendicular iron rod threaded at the top, the hub of the newly made or mended wheel was placed over this and secured with an outsize washer and nut. Flush and immovable it lay on the plate ready to be shod. The smith then produced a simple metal disc which revolved on a handle, called a traveller. This was run around the outside of the wheel and then around the inside of the tyre to measure whether the fit was accurate or how great was the discrepancy.

If the rim was too small it had to be 'stretched'. To do this he would place it on the fire and when it glowed white hot, with the aid of his mate, he lifted it off and placed it on the anvil. Together they hammered with quick, clanging blows and then measured the rim again, which by this time would be about an inch larger in circumference and ready for fitting. Again the tyre had to be heated, the smith and his mate turned it round and round, sweat running down their faces and dripping in rivulets into their open-necked collarless shirts. A piece of wood was rubbed over the tyre - if it was hot enough the wood would smoke and almost smoulder.

Then, gripping the tyre with tongs they carried it outside, lowered it over the waiting wheel and began hammering again, gently in one part, more strongly in another, till it was well fitted. Smoke rose from the scorching wood and blackened the wheel, buckets of water were sloshed round and round the tyre, the air was filled with an acrid smell. Hissing, spitting and fuming like a witch's cauldron, smoke rose so thickly that the smith at the opposite side was completely screened from view. Gradually it subsided, the clouds disappeared and there at their feet lay the wheel, tight enclosed in its tyre.

Shoeing of horses and wheels were not the only jobs done by the blacksmiths. Anything in wrought ironwork from mending a broken fire grate, to the making of decorative iron gates fell within their province. Often an extra pair of hands was needed for lifting and carrying and the smithy was a popular place for the young men to gather and sometimes they earned themselves tuppence with which to buy a drink.

The village boasted nine pubs - more than enough for its population of about one thousand people, and in an attempt to divert the men's leisure to better use, a Mutual Improvement Society set up a Reading Room which was open every evening, except Sundays. There seems to have been little reading or improving done there, but much playing of billiards, snooker, cards and dominoes. The billiard room was upstairs and the card room down below in a sort of cellar.

The Fire Engine

 Well before the First World War, the village invested in a fire-engine, which was housed in a lean-to structure adjoining the Reading Room. It was a hand-worked pump on a light trolley, equipped with a long leather hose fastened all down the side with copper rivets. Charles Wells was the Captain. It was his responsibility to ensure that the engine was always ready for call out and everything on it, axes and the like, were in good order. For this he received £2 a year. Sixteen men of the village were on the roll and in the event of an alarm as many of them as could be mustered would run to the fire-engine shed.

Horses were commandeered from local tradesmen, boys and men ran to fetch them up from the common. With all possible speed two horses would be harnessed to the trolley and away they would dash to the scene of the fire. The hose was fixed to the front part of the engine and the other end was run down to a pond, river or dyke. The men applied vigorous muscle-power to the bars on either side, pumping up and down to draw up the water.

Most of the calls were to burning stacks or chimney fires. One call was to a house on fire at Wroxham, a good two miles away. It must have been well ablaze by the time the Coltishall brigade arrived. Some of the people watching had never seen a fire-engine before and one exclaimed in astonishment - "Cor - look at that! They've brought a piano!" That was just about what the contraption looked like.

On that day the highly equipped Norwich Fire Brigade was also called, but by the time they arrived and laid their hoses all the way to Wroxham bridge (they feared they would soon draw the nearby dyke dry in spite of being told repeatedly by the locals that it was connected to the Broad) the Coltishall Brigade had practically got the blaze under control and the village men received great praise from the house-holder.

There was no fire alarm bell, someone just ran or rode horseback with the message and the men warned one another. Sometimes the call came in the night; with luck and foresight if it was a farmer he might bring a horse or two with him when he called for Mr Wells.

'I remember one night they came after my father and they already had the old horse with them,' recalled Ralph Wells. 'They banged on the door. "Come on, Charlie," they shouted. "We've got a fire at Belaugh Green - Ben Ling's place. We want your engine up there."

'Father, he had to scrap out of bed and he began to pull on his trousers. He was in such a hurry he began to put on the first pair that he got hold of. My mother soon clawed them out of his hand - they were his new Sunday trousers! Cor - she didn't half go on at him! Anyway he soon got another pair and ran down with the key of the fire-shed. There was a pit up there, near the fire, so I think they put that one out all right.'

To pull the fire-engine horses were comandeered from local tradesmen. Here Mr James Spinks (on left) is in charge of the volunteers. (Photo: Gordon Jarvis)

Another fire was almost next door to the fire-engine shed. At that time part of Roy's old shop was thatched and that caught fire, so they called out the engine. It was near enough for the men to push it along without bothering to harness up the horses, but while they were doing this all Roy's men were busy with ladders and biscuit tins and buckets passing water up on a human chain system. The firemen ran their hoses down to the river, began to pump vigorously and lifted the hose ready to direct the jet.

'Where do you want it?' shouted the Captain.

The roof was almost hidden in smoke.

'Too late. You can pump it back where it came from,' was the reply. 'We've already put the fire out.'

Each time they were used, the hoses had to be carted up to the Captain's house in Chapel Lane. There they were cleaned, hung up to dry and the leather oiled to keep it supple and in good condition. They were taken back to the fire-engine shed on a wheelbarrow.

Once a year, on Whit Monday, the brigade put on a display for the village. They pulled the engine across the road and down to the river beside the top common, they pumped and sprayed the water up with their hoses, making huge cascades and fountains, playing them up and down, arching and crossing. It was one of the events of the village year and certainly one the children looked forward to very much. The fire-engine was sold in 1920 and presumably scrapped.

Marl-Digging

 Marl was extensively used in agriculture and enormous quantities were dug from huge pits in Horstead and Coltishall from as far back as the sixteenth century, the industry reaching its peak in the early nineteenth century. Evidence of the extent of these diggings can still be seen in the area known as Little Switzerland.

The marlpits in Coltishall were on the eastern side of the North Walsham Road where, in 1810, several Roman urns were found. Marl-digging had probably only recently commenced there, as the final depth of the pits was about 20 to 30 feet and the urns lay much closer to the surface than that. As the digging continued other urns were found, 14 feet below the surface, in 1850.

At one side of this marl-pit, close to where the Railway Inn now stands is the ruin of a lime-kiln and also a brick-kiln, for this pit yielded not only marl, but also a laminated clay. The flint-studded front of the brick kiln had a deep arched entrance and within was a brick dome, about 24 feet in diameter at floor level. From the centre rose a huge circular chimney in the base of which were six fire-holes. Nowadays the old marlpits are overgrown and make attractive features, but what a scar they must have made on the landscape when they were operating, with their white gleaming sides and all the roads white-dusted as loads were carted about.

Some marl was simply shipped away and spread on the land in its original state of raw chalk, or used to build up the river banks, but much of it was first burnt in the village kilns, for it was well known that 'burnt' lime would improve the land at a much faster rate. In those days lime was also used for the making of mortar, and for hygiene and cleanliness the interiors of kitchens, dairies and other outbuildings were lime-washed. The most extensive lime-kilns were at Gt Hautbois. Chalk was brought there on mule carts and shovelled into the well-stoked kilns which were linked by a series of underground tunnels. The resultant lime was then shovelled into sacks and barrowed along to a shaft over which was a windlass with which the bags were lifted ready to cart to the staithe to load on wherries, or in later years, to the station.

A by-product of the chalk pits was the large number of flint stones which were found in strata through the chalk. These flints were broken up by the roadman who sat on the verge, with a zinc gauze over his face to save his eyes from the flying chips. They were used to mend the roads and their sharp edges were a constant hazard to cyclists and Mr Willie Wilson senior, well known in Wroxham and Coltishall as 'the man from the Pru' - who made all his rounds by bicycle, frequently had cause to curse them as he mended punctures or had to buy new tyres.

Many gardens in the village still possess large hollow flints, acting as natural flower containers or as unusual ornaments, and these too are the product of the marlpits. They are known as pot-stones or paramoudras, and were found by the marl-excavators in vertical lines, deep in the chalk of the pit. They vary in size from about 18 inches to three feet long, and are roughly cylindrical in shape. With their smooth, rounded shapes and holes they closely resemble the work of a modern sculptor.

Building

The building of a new house or a terrace of smaller houses always aroused a great deal of interest in the village. In those days there were no big developers and all building work was carried out by local craftsmen - bricklayers, carpenters, plumbers, glaziers and decorators working independently.

There were two carpenters in Coltishall, both of whom also worked as wheelwrights. Robert Hook's place was in Rectory Road. He lived in Jasmine Cottage, rather smaller then than it is now and he used the barn as his carpenter's shop. Mr Hook had the only steam engine in the village, which must have given him a considerable advantage when it came to sawing up wood, compared with the traditional method of cutting up trees manually over the saw-pit.

The other carpenter, Walter Vout, occupied the triangular site pointing to the bridge. The workshops were alongside the main road through the village, facing the blacksmiths and the remainder of the area was used for storage, chiefly of wood. In those days there were several trees standing on this site, now occupied by petrol pumps, and it was a familiar sight to see long planks of wood, poles and ladders leaning against them.

In the year 1911 young Walter Watts left the village school and began his apprenticeship in this carpenter's yard. His father already worked for Walter Vout and the Watts family had been in the village for at least two hundred years and had mostly been in the building trade. Walter's great-great-grandfather had helped to build the shop that now goes under the name of Cottage Antiques, and put his mark on it with initials in iron 'R.W'. The cottage in which Walter lives now, in retirement, used to belong to his grandfather and he was born in one of the row of five cottages adjoining it, but he does not know which.

Walter's grandfather 'did a bit of cooping and painting and also sold coal'. The coal was shot down into the cellars below the house and the cooper's shop was behind the family living quarters, which consisted of two rooms up and two down with a small kitchen at the back. A good comfortable standard for those days.

When Walter first started at the carpentering trade he was paid half a crown a week and worked from six in the morning till six at night, with a half hour for breakfast and an hour for dinner. They left off at twelve o'clock on Saturdays, summer and winter. One of the first jobs he had was at the bottom end of the saw, in the saw-pit, all day long.

'Hard work for a boy, that was,' he said, remembering even yet the weary ache of overtired young muscles. 'The tree would be there perhaps two or three days - it all depended what you wanted it planked into, and if the wind got up a bit, the sawdust would be falling into your eyes all the time.'

*Cutting
timber into
planks was
slow work
and involved
two men
working in
unison.*

The saw-pit was about 12 to 14 feet long, three and a half to four feet wide with bricked arches. Rough steps led down to the bottom, some six feet deep. 'We used dog-irons - flat at one end and pointed at the other - and rollers to hold the tree firmly on the pit. We drove the flat end of the dog-iron into the tree and the pointed end was driven into the roller to hold it. Then we marked it with a chalk line to make a guide to cut by. If it was a darkish bit of wood we used chalk, but if it was light wood we'd use a bit of burnt poplar.'

The saw itself was very long with a handle placed crosswise at the wider end. The more experienced man stood over the trunk, for he had to guide the saw along the marked line. Walter had to go down into the pit and fix a gadget to the other end of the saw which provided him with a handle. They worked in unison, toiling on and on, cutting each time up to the roller, then starting the next cut, an inch or two along, or whatever thickness of board was needed. When each board had been cut up to the roller, they moved the tree along and continued cutting the boards along the next section until they had planked the whole length of the tree.

The wood was stored under the carpenter's shop, each plank separated by a small spline so that the air could circulate between. Some of it must have lain there ten or twenty years to season before being used to make window-frames, mullions, doors and of course, from time to time, a coffin. A well-seasoned piece of oak was a pleasure for a craftsman to work. A fresh scent of planed timber pervaded the air, the curls of pale golden wood shavings were swept beneath the carpenter's benches. In a corner was the big grindstone for keeping chisels and plane blades razor sharp.

'We only had one horse and cart when I worked at Mr Vout's,' said Walter. 'But they kept another horse, a big strong old fellow he was, for carting the trees home on the gill.' The gill had two huge wheels. 'You had to get the tree and make it balance between. Chains went round on the end, to hold the front so it didn't slide off.

'If we went down a hill, we'd take the horse out at the top, then the men would get on the back of the tree and drag it on the ground. They had to hold it back so it didn't go too fast down the hill. If they'd left the horse in the gill with the heavy tree trunk, it might have run over the horse.' So the trunk dragged along, biting into the rough road surface, and the men guided it down the hill. They fetched only one tree at a time and sometimes brought it five or six miles back to the carpenter's yard.

Timber was also carried on the wherries, and it was not unusual for tree trunks to be stacked on the lower common awaiting shipment by river. If there were too many of them then the villagers would complain to the Lords of the Manor, King's College, Cambridge and at one time it was ordered that timber should be stacked only on a certain part of the green.

A couple of times Walter Watts recalled working on repairs to the water mill which straddled the river, built of white-painted weather-boarding, a high structure rising sheer from brick arches, fifty feet above the swirling water.

'That was a tricky job, that was! We used to have a wherry on the pool side to put our ladders in, to reach the top. The wherry would be tied up to the mill. That was the only way we could get up. When the tide rose the top of the ladder might catch against the weather-board, so you had to be sure you had six or seven inches for the ladder to rise up the boards at the top. Of course, the tide doesn't come up very fast, but you had to watch it while you worked up there.'

The Baker

Another lad who left school at about this time was Ralph Wells, the son of the captain of the fire-brigade, who had sold bloaters for Bob Pike. He went to work at a shop kept by 'Little' Tom Coman (to distinguish him from another of the same name) and Little Tom's two spinster sisters Emma and May.

'I hadn't been there above six months when my oldest brother, who was apprenticed to the basket-maker, was stopped in the street by Harry Hudson, who had just taken over the bakery from his father-in-law, Mr Hunt. Harry Hudson asked my brother "How much does young Ralph get at that shop?"

' "I don't know. Not a lot, I expect."

'Mr Hudson, he say - "I wonder if he'd like to come and work for me?"

'So of course, my brother he told me about that and that was how I went into the bakery trade and I worked there until I retired - apart from my time away in the war.

'There were six or seven men working at the Bakery. Some were Coltishall men, but a couple of them came from Foulsham and lodged in the village.

The bakers. Harry Hudson is standing third from right. Ralph Wells is standing on the left and Billy Buck is seated right, with Cecil Coman behind him.

'Before R.J.Read took over the mill it belonged to Ben Barwood. He also owned the bakery in Coltishall and whoever hired the bakery had to buy all their flour from the mill.

'I worked as baker and roundsman, both. We used to be up early in the morning-or all night come to that at Easter, making Hot Cross Buns. You'd be working in the sweating heat in the bakery and then you'd go out in a wind frost in the horse and cart - you'd think it'd be enough to kill anybody!

'On a Saturday I'd load up with bread, flour, and a few buns and leave the bakery at about 11 a.m. making calls all the way down Coltishall Street, starting at the little shop opposite the church, Libby Wright's. Then on down Anchor Street, by the boatyards and the maltings, back to the Wroxham Road and then drive straight to Horning, about six or seven miles away. I called on the houses in Horning street and along as far as Horning Ferry. I only went to the Ferry in the summer, because the old lady who lived there, Mrs Crowe, took in visitors for the holiday season. The ferry was working in those days, a sort of punt attached to a chain by which you could be pulled over the river.'

The children of Horning knew better than to chant to Ralph, as they did to the passing 'gentry' on their pleasure wherries. 'Please get your coppers ready,' advised Ernest Suffling 'For, as the village is being passed, a crowd of noisy little lads and lasses will run along the bank singing.

'Ho, John Barleycorn! Ho, John Barleycorn!

All day long I raise my song

No, John Barleycorn!'

'The children created great fun for the passing holiday-makers in scrambling for any coppers that were thrown to them. The origin of the song is unknown, but apparently even three-year-old toddlers joined in and the general effect was said to be pleasing.

Ralph Wells had no time or cash to indulge in such frivolity - though perhaps some of the pennies that were picked up might be spent on buns from his cart. They were two-wheeled carts in those days, the goods covered by a white tilt, but the roundsman sat out in all weathers. Later they had four-wheeled vans, with an awning over the driver's seat which kept off some of the weather.

'We had to look after our own vans and make sure the lamps were in order, cleaned and filled with paraffin or candles.'

Ralph's route lay back through Horning Street, up Ropes Hill and on past Neatishead windmill. On he went, the horse plodding along with the wheels of the high van grinding on the gravelled roads, right through Water Lane, the greater part of which is now scarcely distinguishable, lost in a tangle of brambles and untended fallen trees.

'I'd go to Neatishead Street, call at Beeston Hall and Hoveton Hall and then home. That was a good day's work I can tell you. When I got back to Coltishall I still had to look after the horse, unharness him and rub him down and give him food and water. We each had our own horse, stabled behind the bakery.

'The bread was baked in a coal oven, a double-decker, made in Cardiff, a

Ralph Wells, driving his horse Jolly, on his last round before retirement, about 1960. (Photo: Stan Sinclair)

wonderful old oven, packed with asbestos for keeping the heat in. Every Monday morning we used to make hollow biscuits. We'd be there together, all us blokes, the bakers. Old Ted Coman, he'd be in the corner of the bake office with a pair of scales and his job was to weigh up. He'd cut off a bit of dough, nip off a little piece if it was too big - each bit had to be exactly one ounce. He'd give it a bit of a roll and throw the pieces over to us chaps and we'd have to pull them in halves and round them up, like you would a marble and put them on a board.

'When we'd got a board full we would hand that over to another bench and the guv'nor, old Harry Hudson, he'd have a scraper, a flat thing with a handle on it and he'd knock them out. The next bloke in the chain had a pricker and he used to prick each of these biscuits and the last man put them on the baking sheets.' The biscuits were then ready to prove and when they had doubled in size they were ready to go into the oven. 'Norfolk hollow biscuits were very well known - we used to sell a lot of them and send them all over the place - some were even sent away by post regularly.'

Motor vans took over the bread delivery in the nineteen thirties, but Ralph never did take to driving one. He stuck to the old way, with Jolly his horse, until he retired.

Basket-Maker and Gardener

Mr Willie Wilson recalled that when he left school his first job was at the basket-makers and thatchers. Their name was Thixton and their house, set close to the river was swept away in the flood of 1912. The Thixtons were relatives of Willie's so it was natural that they should take him on as an apprentice, but he never really took to the work.

'I didn't mind the thatching too much, but I didn't like having to sit down trying to make baskets. I never did get the hang of basket-making. Everyone used baskets in those days, for fetching and carrying; on the farms they had skeps for carrying mangols to the cattle and tall skeps, about four feet deep for chaff; there were butcher's baskets, and baker's baskets, shopping baskets and baskets for the delivery boys' bikes, baskets for bloaters, cradles for the babies and bees hives too. I even heard of a basket coffin, specially made for some local eccentric. He wouldn't be carried along the road, they had to carry him across the fields to Hautbois Church. That was his wish, and that was what they did.'

The extent of basket-making in the village is revealed year by year in the School Log Book in the 1870s. Every April and May there was a considerable fall in attendance. 'Osier peeling,' wrote the headmaster. 'Children either working or taking meals to their mothers, brothers, and sisters who are so engaged.'

In about 1913 Willie Wilson left the basket-makers and went to work for Mrs Rogers at Coltishall Hall, as a gardener. They employed about four gardeners then, plus the Head Gardener. Willie was paid ten shillings a week. A year or so later he moved to Horstead Hall, hoping to better himself for, not only did he earn two shillings a week more, but being a gardener at Horstead Hall was said to be such good training that it was a stepping stone to a job at one of the really grand gardens, such as Blickling Hall.

'The lads who worked in the garden lived in a bothy. It was a small brick place, with one room down where we could have a fire and boil up a meal, heat the soup we'd fetched from home or anything like that, and another room upstairs where we slept.' He shared it with another lad. They had to find all their own food. He was there till he went into the army in 1916 at the age of 17.

The Village in the Mid-Nineteenth Century.

 The population of Coltishall grew considerably during the nineteenth century, not only because of the increased birthrate, which was general throughout the country, but also because of people moving in, mostly from smaller villages nearby. In 1801, when the first census was made there were 601 inhabitants, but forty years later this had increased by almost fifty per cent. In those days, when many could not read or write, enumerators were appointed whose task was to fill in the details of each family.

In 1841 two enumerators were appointed for Coltishall and Gt Hautbois - one of whom was John Field. He was in his mid-thirties and kept the grocery shop now known as Church Stores. He rented pastures between the church and the river and behind Grove House, so one may assume he had horses, but whether he rode to the further away areas of the village or completed his task on foot we cannot tell. The other enumerator, William Coman, was a schoolmaster, aged about sixty. In meticulously clear handwriting he compiled the census for Hautbois Magna and 'all that part of Coltishall lying south of the road from the river to Belaugh.' From their reports we can discover something of the commercial and domestic life of the village at that time.

John Field started his survey opposite the church, calling at the home of James Coman, aged 30, who lived with his wife Deborah and two small children. Next he called upon John Clements, a carpenter, whose eldest son at 14 was already apprenticed to his father. Then came an agricultural labourer, a lady hat-maker, a shoemaker and a bricklayer in whose house were two lodgers, both agricultural workers. Quite a number of young men lodged at various houses in the village.

John visited Ann Codling, an octogenarian, who lived with Isabella Steward, aged 65 and twenty-years old Sarah Steward. Close by was Susannah Bendy, aged 70, of independent means and next Miss Ann Ansell, also aged 70, the daughter of a respected family of boat-owners. Her companion was Maria Roberts.

In the next five households, in Culley's Yard, the breadwinners were all agricultural labourers; then came a glazier, a journeyman painter and after that John Field entered his own household. There is no mention of a wife but he had three children under the age of ten, two elderly ladies lived with him and two young female servants.

After listing three more families of agricultural labourers, he turned from Church Street and walked through Chapel Lane - at that time called Postle's Lane after a well-known local brewer - to begin his survey of St

James. There again several families of agricultural labourers were crowded into the small cottages whilst at Belaugh Green was Henry Mayes, a tenant farmer, respected and well-to-do. Also in St James was the boatbuilder, Robert Kerrison, a butcher named Spooner Fitt and the veterinary surgeon, George Limmer, whose wife was called Mahala; they had five children aged from two to 15.

Daniel Moore kept the White Lion Inn and also worked as a watch-maker. The blacksmith at St James was John Cook and his eldest son at 15 was apprenticed to his father's trade, whilst the younger boy, George was an agricultural labourer. On the island site, at the junction of White Lion Road and Belaugh Green were four families of agricultural labourers and close by old Emma Cooper, aged 85 and Hannah Cadge, both of independent means. There was also a wine merchant with his wife, son and two unmarried daughters all living at home plus a servant girl, Maria Coman.

John Field then walked on to Lyng common and there and at Potspoon Holes were six families of agricultural labourers with about 18 children under 15, plus five youths who also worked on the land. After taking in those far flung areas John called on the 'squire' at Coltishall Hall. The Rev James Ward, aged 70, was in Holy Orders but had sufficient means not to need to hold a living. His wife Maria was about the same age and living in was one male servant and four female servants. Close by were two gardeners and two laundresses. John then walked back up the hill towards the cluster of houses opposite the church where he had started his day's enumerating, presumably to pick up those folk who had not been at home earlier. He listed three more families of labourers and a journeyman carpenter.

His next call was at the schoolhouse, where Henry Massingham at only 25 years old was the school-master, helped by his wife, Ann, and by his father who lived nearby. There John listed the names of 14 boarders aged between six and 15. There was one female servant, Maria Sizor, aged 20 who must have been kept pretty busy.

There were a few more big families of agricultural labourers and then, coming to the heart of the village, he picked up some of the small businessmen - tailors, harnessmakers, shoemakers, shopkeepers, carpenters, coopers and a plumber. At the Grove was Ann Pightling, of independent means, whilst John Law, the aptly named police officer, lodged with a retired army officer. The carrier was John Barnard who went to Norwich three times a week. The blacksmith, James Reeve, lived close to where the car showrooms now stand and there were two families of Tunmore who both worked as bricklayers. John then called on his fellow enumerator, William S.Coman, who lived with his daughter, Maria.

At the Old House was Elizabeth Hawes, the young widow of Robert Hawes a wealthy brewer who had died in March of that same year, leaving her with three small children aged three, one and four months. She had one man-servant and five female servants, the youngest of whom was 13 years old Charlotte Smith. Elizabeth Hawes senior, aged 85, lived at Coltishall House with four servants, a man, a boy of 12 and two females. She was also a widow and her eldest son, Siday, with his wife, Barbara, seven children and four female servants occupied The Mead. The Hawes were among the richest people in the village, making their money from malting and brewing and their three large households employed 14 live-in servants and undoubtedly provided work for many others.

The Coltishall Brewery Estate was auctioned in September 1841 and the four-day sale included 53 inns and public houses. Robert Hawes was only 48 when he died, and he had been unique in building up a considerable collection of ale houses, well before most brewers had caught on to the idea of tied houses. His brewery buildings and one of his malthouses were clustered around his home at the Old House; the second malthouse was across the road and alongside it was the stable block for 12 horses. There the heavy shires rested between hauling their drays loaded with barrels of beer to pubs at Catton, Blofield, Ludham, North Walsham, Cromer, Aylsham and many places in between, or of course, to the river to be transported by wherry.

William Coman was the enumerator who called at The Mead and he then continued his walk down Wroxham Road where in the next cluster of habitations lived a saddler, a butcher, a waterman and several families of agricultural labourers. John Burrell kept the Kings Head Inn and two middle-aged ladies ran the grocery shop. In Anchor Street were the boat-builders Thomas Wright and Samuel Press; landlord at the Anchor was Charles King; there were also watermen, a couple more carpenters, a cooper and three maltsters. Strangely there were more maltings than there were maltsters.

In all John Field called at 138 houses and listed 645 people. William Coman called on 48 houses in Coltishall and listed another 243 people, bringing the total population of the village to 897. There were six empty houses, no one sleeping rough and no one had recently emigrated to foreign parts. The census report also shows that only about half the people then living in Coltishall had been born there. People from all walks of life had moved in and settled, the majority of whom were born within the county, only five per cent having been born elsewhere.

Children and young people under the age of 15 accounted for a very large proportion of the population. Most girls in the age band 15 to 19 were employed as servants in the village households and many continued to be so employed, unless married, into their early twenties. Many went to service in London, for Norfolk girls had a reputation for being good and loyal employees.

A total of 81 men and boys were listed as agricultural labourers, and five simply as labourers, but these terms are misleading for undoubtedly they were used very loosely to categorise every farm worker and many others also. Only one man gave his occupation as groom and one as an ostler - yet there must have been many whose work included specialised skills in the care of horses, cows or pigs and whose prowess in ploughing, reaping, or stacking should have been worthy of more recognition. From Mary Hardy's diary, written while she lived at The Limes from 1773 to 1781, the variety of work done by the labourers is apparent. For example 'men began plowing for wheat - jobbing about at home - brewing - in malthouse - mending hedges - began wetting the barley.' The expertise involved was taken for granted as when the 'Great Red Cow took Bull', or when 'the sow pigg'd.' From boyhood the labourers learned all those many skills that were necessary on the farm and in its allied industries.

At the other end of the social scale there were 28 persons of independent means who no doubt varied from the affluent to those who managed in a rather genteel poverty on rents from the cottages, or small annuities. Living-in staff for the big households accounted for 38 female servants and six men. Those households would also have employed the six gardeners and probably availed themselves of the services of the dress-makers, laundresses and the hat-maker. The watch-maker, in addition to making a variety of timepieces, including grandfather clocks, went the rounds of the big houses once a week to wind up their clocks.

In Coltishall five men were listed by the census report as farmers, but these do not include those principal owners of the soil directly designated as of independent means, who could have added 'gentleman farmer' to their occupations. Farming was still mostly labour intensive and the old ways were still very much used, even by progressive farmers, but experimentation was going on apace, and new machinery was coming in such as drills and threshing-machines. As far as I can discover this change over took place peacefully in Coltishall - I have read of no resistance among the workforce to new methods.

The Palgraves

King's College, Cambridge was (and still is) 'Lord of the Manor' and at that time owned the Manor House. From the middle of the 18th century this property was leased to Captain Thomas Palgrave (1715-1775) and then to his son William (1745-1822). The Palgraves were merchants in corn, coal and shipping and carried on their business in Great Yarmouth as well as in Coltishall.

Born at Great Yarmouth, Thomas Palgrave served an apprenticeship at sea and rose to the rank of captain. He displayed such courage and ability that he was given command of a privateer, sailing under 'Letters of Marque' which authorised him to attack the ships of hostile nations. His first voyage was unsuccessful as he met with a much larger French vessel, was forced to surrender, and held as a prisoner of war for some years.

When he returned to Yarmouth once again he supervised the building of another privateer and took its command. On this voyage also he was beaten by superior odds but returned undaunted, obtained a third command and this time met with success, captured several rich prizes and amassed a small fortune. With this he was able to retire from the sea whilst only in his late thirties. For some years he lived in London, where he became one of the Elder Brethren of Trinity House and a Director of Greenwich Hospital. In

NORFOLK BROADS
THE MANOR HOUSE, COLTISHALL.

FOR SALE BY PRIVATE TREATY.—A beautifully-situated GEORGIAN RESIDENCE, containing three fine reception rooms, ten bedrooms, two bathrooms. Mains electricity, two hot-water systems, etc. Billard room. Garage for 3 cars, spacious Outbuildings, Gardener's Cottage. Delightful gardens, two fine tennis courts, Dutch garden, rock and water garden, Stone-paved quay-heading and boathouse, with long frontage to a lovely unspoiled reach of the River Bure. In all about 16 ACRES. Freehold. Low outgoings. VACANT POSSESSION. £3,150.

J. R. E. DRAPER, Land Agent, Wroxham.

From the middle of the 18th century the Manor House was leased by Captain Thomas Palgrave, followed by his son William. They were wealthy merchants in corn, coal and shipping. This advertisement is from a magazine of 1937.

about 1750 he bought the lease of the Manor House at Colishall, where he lived for the rest of his life and was buried in the church there.

He always had a rapier in his bedroom to use as a defence against thieves and also kept a rope ladder coiled up under his bed to enable him to escape out of the window in case of fire. In 1837 he married Mary Manning, who came from an well-known Yarmouth family and they had four children but sadly three of them died in infancy. He was succeeded at the Manor House by his only surviving son.

William Palgrave inherited not only from his father, but also from his uncle, another William Palgrave, who died in 1780. In this way he held estates in both Great Yarmouth and Coltishall, but he made the Manor House his principal residence. He was a Whig and took an active part in the politics of Great Yarmouth where he was Mayor in 1782 and again in 1805. He was an ardent supporter of Thomas Coke of Holkham and was frequently a guest at his celebrated annual sheep-shearing.

He was also very interested in farming and enjoyed experimenting with new farming methods, listing his results with care. He sowed some barley by drilling and some by broadcasting and found that he got as much barley from two bushels drilled as from four broadcast, whilst on wheat his best results were obtained by dibbling. He improved his meadows by spreading sea-sand from Yarmouth, which killed all sedge and rushes and brought up a fine sheet of white clover. He also brought up by wherry large quantities of sea-ouze or haven-mud and found it beneficial on dry scalding gravels and sands, where it formed a cool bottom. However he was not always so successful, for when he used 'moory-mud from the bottom of the river, mixed with lime and marl' it produced a profusion of weeds, especially persicaria. This troublesome weed has pink flowers and its leaves carry a large black blotch, said to be the mark of the devil.

One of the richest men in the village at that time, William Palgrave could afford to experiment. His estate was sold at auction on 7th September 1822 when he retired from business and then consisted of several excellent dwelling houses, including The Mead, and Holly Lodge, with gardens, offices and out-buildings, adapted for the residence of genteel families. Also there were cottages said to be 'well worth the attention of persons desirous to secure votes'(for in those days only house-holders of property of an annual value of 40 shillings or more were entitled to vote).

The Manor House was advertised as a most valuable leasehold estate, possessing every accommodation for a respectable family, commanding a delightful view over a considerable tract of rich and well-timbered pastures. It had a large garden, well stocked with the best fruit trees and thriving plantations. The mercantile buildings consisted of a counting-house, malthouse, malt mill, granaries, brewery, wine vault, cinder ovens, coal yard, hay-house, chaise-house, cart-lodge and granary, bullock shed, cow-houses, piggeries, four stables and other buildings necessary to a concern of magnitude. The situation was said to be one of the finest in the county for a merchant, with a large and commodious staithe where an extensive business in the corn and coal trade had been carried on for more than seventy years.

The Poor

One of the inducements listed in the sale particulars of the estate of William Palgrave in 1822 was that the 'Poor's rates are moderate.' Indeed in 1801 the Poor's rate in Coltishall was 1/6d which certainly compared favourably with North Walsham at 4/- and Scottow at 16/- whilst the average was for the area was about 5/6d.

The Overseer's Book reveals that about 50 cottagers were regularly unable to pay their rates through poverty, but there were sufficient fairly rich people to provide an average of well over £500 a year for disbursement within the village and regular weekly payments were made to between 40 and 50 people. More than half of these were widows and other poor women; about a dozen illegitimate children were also supported (the Baptism Register shows about 1 entry in 8 as being illegitimate) whilst the men who received benefit were mostly too old or infirm to work. These weekly payments averaged a little over £200 a year and another £300 plus was spent on 'Need money and bills'. These included the clerk's salary of £8, travelling, maintaining the Town House for two large families, payments to the sick, pauper's burials, Asylum bills, surgeon's bills and clothes for girls going into service, and passes for vagrants.

One very extraordinary entry reads - 'August 7th 1820 - Passes for 32 women and 192 children, 5th Regiment of Foot - £7. 6. 5d' The 5th Regiment of Foot subsequently became the Royal Northumberland Fusiliers, but I have been unable to discover positively why this large number of people should have been wandering through Coltishall at that date. The Regiment sailed for the West Indies on 4th February 1819 and it has been suggested that those remaining in the depot, about 4 officers and 100 men, might have been engaged on a recruiting drive in Norfolk and on their way northwards. In any event the village supported the women and children for that night.

The poor, or perhaps more accurately, the underpaid were certainly there in large numbers and the rich enjoyed being bountiful. On the occasion of the Golden Jubilee of King George III in 1809, a collection amounting to £17. 12s was distributed among the Poor Inhabitants, viz 325 persons, who each received one pound of beef and a 4d loaf.

Dr Grapes also records that 'to celebrate peace on 24th June 1814, 400 inhabitants, led by two natives who had fought by the side of our immortal Nelson' marched behind a martial band to a field where they sat down to a meal of roast beef. This was carried in beneath a banner with the inscription 'Peace to the world - Plenty to the Poor' and was served by the ladies and gentlemen of the parish. After the meal many loyal toasts were pledged in 'the Amber', each accompanied by a discharge of artillery, the ringing of bells and the playing of well selected tunes. The event finished with foot-racing, stick-jumping, diving into a bowls of flour and grinning matches which 'afforded great amusement.' In that last competition, one performer was said to be so adept in the act, that the contending parties speedily resigned the prizes. The celebration ended with a spectacular firework display.

Schools

Long before the passing of the Education Act in 1870, there were several private schools in Coltishall though only a very small proportion of village children benefitted from this. Dr C.Grapes, the rector of both Coltishall and Horstead from 1786 to 1815 recorded the following facilities available in 1808.

Mr H.Osborn, who ran a school in what is now the Old Schoolhouse, had 40 board and day boys, eight girls, and ten village lads who were educated free under a bequest made in his will by John Chapman in 1718. (Before the schoolhouse was built these boys were taught in the church or chancel). Mr Osborn's pupils learned writing, reading and arithmetic, Latin, French and drawing. Mary Hardy's son attended this school as a day boy before going on to the Paston School at North Walsham.

Mr Coman (the one who made the census report) together with his wife ran a school attended by 45 boys and girls. They were taught writing, reading, arithmetic, sewing and knitting.

At Mrs Lucy Neve's school girls learned writing, reading and the use of the needle. Miss Lydia Boorn had three boarders and 19 day girls, whilst Mary Ebbage, the wife of the blacksmith had nine scholars who in addition to reading, sewing and knitting learned to plait straw for hats. Sewing was a very useful accomplishment for girls, not only for the well-being of their own families but so that they might aspire to better positions when they went into service.

In 1814 Mrs Hawes, the wife of the brewer, Siday Hawes senior, also ran a school. She was the sister of Richard Porson, a professor of Greek at Cambridge, so one may assume she was an educated woman and that her school was a philanthropic service. It was held in an upstairs room over the carpenter's shop opposite the Old House when she then lived.

The present attractive, knapped flint school was built by public subscription in about 1840 and was originally known as the Endowed School. In 1845 it became known as the National School and the building previously used was converted into the teacher's house. It was stated to be 'for the education of children of the labouring and other poorer classes in Coltishall and Hautbois Major and for no other purpose.'

The first master was Benjamin Sutton and all boys in Coltishall of the age of six years and upwards, being of good character and health were entitled to admission. There is no mention of girls, but undoubtedly some went also. Fees were to be not less than two pence nor more than sixpence per week and in addition scholars had to pay for their own stationery.

Such expense must have been beyond the means of many families, not all of whom attended. It is interesting to note however, in the register of marriages, that even in the 1830s more than half the population were able to

Form 4 of Coltishall School in 1904. Willie Wilson is second from the right in the front row.(Photo: Connie Wilson)

sign their names, including many who were labourers and the children of labourers.

Richard Bond in his book on Coltishall reveals the ill-will with which compulsory schooling was at first received in the village - and the hostility shown to William Harper, headmaster at the end of the last century. He is described as 'kind and dedicated'. Mr J.G. Walton, who followed him, may also have been dedicated but to some of his pupils he was anything but kind.

'Mr Walton was b- strict,' recalled Ralph Wells. 'He'd cane you across the fingers for the least little thing.'

All the village children went to the one school and each paid a penny a week. There were about eight classes and the part on the east side of it was the infant's section. Miss Balls, the infant's mistress, lived in the house next door. The part that is now the kitchen was the toddler's classroom.

All the boys say they had the cane many a time - and some of the girls had it too. Good attendance was encouraged by the presentation of picture cards - miniature postcards about 3ins by 2ins with black and white views on one side and on the other was printed 'Never absent, never late - week ending:- ' The child's name was written in and the card was stamped by the master. Several former pupils still have a stack of these postcards, which were considerably prized.

Willie Wilson said 'We nearly all got the 'never absent, never late cards' because if there was measles or chickenpox, or diphtheria or anything like that so many children caught it that they closed the whole school. I got cards over most of the weeks I was there during seven years of schooling from the age of 5 to 12. So did my brother. I got one or two medals for attendance too.

With chagrin Willie Wilson also recalled that one never-to-be-forgotten day Mr Walton sent him to the shop to buy a new cane, because some boy had snatched the old one away from him and broken it. Obediently little Willie Wilson carried out his errand, smart in his dark suit and fresh celluloid collar. Cheeks flushed from hurrying, he handed the new cane to the master.

Mr Walton took it and said - 'Well, as you've brought it, you may as well be the first to try it out.'

He gave the boy a cut across the hand, an injustice which not surprisingly, still rankled seventy years later. On another occasion young Willie was caned for wearing the wrong colour of tie.

'There must have been an election coming up and some of the girls had taken to going to school with hair-ribbons in the colours of the Liberals or the Tories. The master said this practice was to stop, but I was quite young, politics didn't mean anything to me.

'I went to school next day, as usual I was always very neat, with a collar and tie - but apparently it was the colour of one of the political parties. I don't know which one. It meant nothing to me, but I got caned for wearing it. I felt that was most unfair.'

Ralph Wells said - 'If you were talking to the boy sitting next to you, you'd be called out. You'd get the cane once, across your fingers, but if you shuffled your feet as you went back to your place, he'd call you back. He was a north countryman with quite a strong accent - at least it was quite noticeable to me.

' "Cum back," he'd say. "Cum back, and have another little bit."

'Then he'd give you a couple more swipes with the cane across your fingers.

' "Never cry," my brothers used to say to me. "No matter how hard he hit you, don't cry. If you do he'll think he's got you beat."

'I never used to cry.

'There were three brothers - Tom, Jack and Steven and if one of them was called out, they'd all go together. They'd try to stand up to the old schoolmaster - but they didn't always get their own way. I've seen him get all three of them on the floor at once and give 'em all a hiding.

'It was mostly reading, writing and arithmetic, that sort of thing. When we got older we used to do a bit of gardening. I suppose Mr Walton was a good schoolmaster really. I think there was more discipline when I was a boy.'

Mary Wells added 'I think we were happier in our childhood than most folks are these days. We were poorer but what we had was good.'

None of the former pupils however, seemed to think that schooldays were the best days of their lives.

Sundays

 Almost all the children in the village attended Sunday School - Church, Salvation Army, Methodist or Wesleyan, each denomination had its own. Church Sunday School was held in the school itself and after the children had been to that, they were expected to go to church but were allowed to leave just before the sermon. Ralph Wells said 'Most of us boys used to go to Sunday School but then we'd go off to play. Sometimes our sister would tell.

' "Father," she'd say. "Them boys never come to church."

'Then he'd tune us up. I think parents used to send us to get us out of the way, not so many of them went to church themselves. My father, he only went once a year. I'll tell you what he used to do. All us kids from Sunday School, we'd sit up in the gallery, where the bell-ringers go in. We all had to sit up there and they always had an old man to sit there along with us, in case we didn't behave ourselves.

'This old man, George Daniels, he had a week's holiday once a year. Then my father took over George Daniels' job - that was how he used to go to church once a year. We certainly had to behave ourselves and go to church that day! We used to be scared stiff that Sunday when our old man went, in case he should catch us up to something.'

Each Sunday School had an annual outing to the seaside, either Bacton or Mundesley. Pupils, teachers and a few mothers all trundled along in wagons provided by local farmers and tradesmen. A date had to be fixed wihich did not interfere with harvest so that wagons, horses and drivers could be loaned for the day. The school supplied wooden forms for the travellers to sit on.

Billy Allen's Sunday School always went to an inn overlooking the sea at Mundesley, where accommodation was provided for the horses and a room set aside for dinner and tea, also for use if it turned out to be wet, which seldom seemed to happen.

'Immediately on our arrival a dash would be made to a neighbouring tuck shop to spend the few pence given to us by parents and friends. Between then and dinner we played on the sand, paddled in the sea and imagined we were helping the fishermen to beach their boats when they came in from a fishing expedition. For dinner we went to the room to eat the sandwiches we had brought and to have soft drinks handed out to us.

'After dinner the teachers organised games and races for which small prizes were awarded. At tea time we again went to the room where a full tea was provided. The sumptuous efforts and the day in the fresh air made most of us tired and many a child was fast asleep by the time the wagons rumbled back into Coltishall.'

Up-Town and Down-Town

Some time ago Coltishall was styled as a town, though it never had a market. The word 'town' survived at least to the end of the nineteenth century, chiefly by such phrases as going 'up-town' or 'down-town' as the case might be. The church was always accepted as marking the division between up and down-town, and this tradition was kept alive by the boys in a spirit of friendly - and sometimes not so friendly - rivalry.

Out of school hours the children had nowhere to play. There were no playing fields and the commons were given over to animals so the roads were the scene of most of their activities. Between the end of afternoon school and the usual tea-time of about six o'clock, there were frequent so-called fights between the boys of 'Up' and 'Downtown.'

The nature of these fights and the weapons used depended on the season. After an appreciable fall of snow and if the snow was in good condition for making snowballs, these fights became fairly common in the vicinity of the church. 'It must be confessed,' wrote Billy Allen 'that some of the snowballs were so closely pressed together that they might more correctly be called iceballs.'

Walter Watts, who was one of the up-town lads, recalled once 'That was winter and the snow was all about. We was snowballing and we drove the down-town boys back as far as the top of the hill and then some of them got pitch-forks and come back at us. We scattered back up the hill then! I remember that well. I don't know why we were separated like that, up-town and down-town - we didn't have the same sort of feud against the Horstead boys in the adjoining village, but in Coltishall itself we were always fighting.'

In summer there were also some fights, but sticks were used as weapons. The results were then sometimes more painful than those in winter. The fights were very fierce while they lasted and at times, in the heat of battle, tempers became somewhat frayed. However, there were certain rules that were usually adhered to.

The school stood in the up-town area, beyond the church and that meant that if a down-towner was kept in after school hours, he would have to pass through enemy territory to reach his own side. It was therefore an unwritten law that he should be allowed passage without molestation, unless he himself showed any evidence of fight. This law was seldom broken. Looking back Billy Allen was surprised to remember that 'in spite of the uproar our fights occasioned, I cannot recall any complaints from residents before whose very doorsteps the skirmishes took place. I imagine them saying "boys will be boys" and leaving it at that. Though the fights took place in one of the main streets through the village, seldom were they interrupted by passing vehicles. How impossible would such horseplay be today.

Leap-Frog, Marbles and 'Stags'

 In winter, when the road was snow-covered and frost had made the surface slippery, it was the custom to make a slide on the edge of the road opposite the school. At times the slide stretched from near the church almost to the house of the Mead gardener. There was no question of up or down town about this, it was a friendly competition to see who could go furthest without mishap.

In the playground behind the school, one of the most popular games with the older boys was leap-frog. There was but one back-maker at any time, an unenviable position which was initially chosen by lot. The game began by all the boys making their leaps from a pre-arranged mark. When each player had made his leap successfully, in the opinion of the leader, who was generally the convenor of the game, the back would be instructed to move a few feet further from the mark. The distance was measured by the back placing his feet heel to toe the requisite number of times. The leapers were not allowed to cross the mark with their feet before leaping. If there were again no failures, the back would be instructed to move still further from the mark and the leader would announce that a jump, hop or stride could be taken before leaping. The leap was now getting more difficult but if everyone got over successfully, the back would move a few feet further and the leader might decree that two of the movements already mentioned could be taken before actually leaping.

'Seldom did the distance have to be increased again,' wrote Billy Allen. 'Failures were almost sure to happen, even before the game reached this stage. Failure was deemed to have occurred if a leaper crossed the line except as instructed, or if he did not make a clean leap over the back. The boy who failed had to take the place of the back and the game began again from the original mark. We often returned to our classrooms much damaged.

'In the front playground less strenuous games were played. They included ordinary leap-frog, conkers and marbles. Marbles came in three varieties. The 'donee' was the lowest grade of marble, being but imperfectly rounded pieces of baked clay. Higher in the scale were the painted professionally produced type of marble and higher still was the much prized glass alley.

'When several games of marbles were in progress, there might suddenly arise a cry of 'fuzzee'. At once the players would make a rush to grab their marbles, for this cry meant a raider was on the way. He would collect as many marbles as he could. This was not really regarded as theft, but rather as an unwelcome occurence in the game. In fact the raider himself was often the originator of the warning cry.

Another pastime which recognised no feud between up and down town was carried out further afield. The scene of this activity was well within down town and was called stags. Those taking part assembled by the church, as was usual with most schoolboy activities. Two boys were selected as stags and in accordance with another of those unwritten rules, they were allowed time to reach Chapel Lane, almost out of sight of the church, before the hounds, as the rest of the players were called, set off in pursuit.

The stags proceeded to the other end of the lane and along the footpath bordering an arable field known as the 'Eight Acres'. This led to a stretch of grazing land intersected by a small wood called 'The Carr'. Once the stags reached this they were entitled to go wherever they pleased, except on neighbouring arable fields, but if the hounds were at a total loss as to which direction to take, they would call and one or other of the stags had to give audible notice of their position. Immediately the hounds would dash off in the direction indicated but the stags would do their best to change their position.

'There was plenty of exercise,' said Billy Allen. What with dashing across the grass, through the wood or crossing the shallow brook that ran alongside the wood. I am afraid we often went home with sodden boots and stockings, because the brook was a little too wide for most of us to jump. When the hounds got sight of a stag, then came a great chase, but capture was not completed until the stag was firmly held or even sat upon.

'Time passed quickly and if it became imperative to make tracks for home before both stags were caught, the hounds would acknowledge failure by giving a shout signifying their abandonment of the chase.'

A Child at the Manor House

Quite different from this rough and tumble was the life of little Dorothy Lake, whose grandmother rented the Manor House from 1882 to 1890. Dorothy was about six years old when she first came there for her summer holidays, accompanied by her brother. From the first she found the grounds beside the river a great joy, and many a time she stood to watch the majestic passing of the wherries. She and her brother were each given a small patch of garden where she grew flowers and her brother grew vegetables. It was obviously a lovely change from London where the family occupied a large house and where she attended a private school. At Coltishall Dorothy kept a large family of dolls and several books which were different and separate from those she had at her London home.

Writing her reminiscences in the 1920s, by which time she had become Mrs Dorothy Kingsbury, she recalled some of the people she had known in the village. These were the Birkbecks of Horstead Hall; the Archdales, quite a large family who lived at Grove House; Admiral Sir John Corbett, an antiquarian scholar whose wife and family gave little Dorothy her first lesson in rowing. She knew the Rogers of Coltishall Hall, 'old Tom Gorell' who was then in his nineties and his daughter, Jane. There was an eccentric old Miss Weston, whose house and grounds were entirely surrounded by a very high black wooden paling 'so that no-one should ever catch an expected glimpse of her'. Two of the servants were especially remembered, named 'Norgate' and Mrs Roberts, the latter an excellent cook, who no doubt made some specially tasty dishes for the little miss.

'I have never forgotten Coltishall church on Sundays, or the curate called Smelt, whose name left an indelible impression on my youthful mind. I can also vividly recall the voice of the old clerk who droned out the responses of the litany in monotonous monotones and whose entreaty We beseech Thee to "air" us, Good Lord, carried one mentally to the domicile of the village laundress. I always listened with rapt attention and interest for the change from Good Lord deliver us, to the "airing" supplication.'

In the hallway of the Manor House were two tigerskin rugs, trophies of her uncle Paston's shooting expeditions in India, which lay on the floor, mouths open, displaying cruel looking teeth. When Dorothy's tiny fingers explored the forehead of one of these tiger skins she could feel with a delicious shudder the hole where the rifle bullet had penetrated the skull. Those skins stirred her imagination to visions of thrilling adventures in the jungle. There was also a glass fire-screen, filled with small gaily coloured tropical birds which enchanted the little girl.

Among the books kept for Dorothy at Coltishall were *A Very Simple Story* by Florence Montgomery which always made her cry when she read it, and the equally touching *Misunderstood* by the same author.

'I can never forget the melancholy feeling which overshadowed everything I did during the last few days of my visits to Coltishall! To say goodbye to my beloved Aunt Margaret and to exchange cheerfully the delights of Coltishall for the dingy grimness of London streets was well-nigh intolerable.' But all too soon the Great Eastern Railway whirled her back to the metropolis.

One big excitement of Dorothy's memories was when in 1885 her Aunt Katherine was married to Mr A.C.Radcliffe. 'It was an event at which I, then aged eight, felt of considerable importance, being one of the bridesmaids. My fellow bridesmaid was another little girl of about my own age, Nellie Somers-Smith, a niece of the bridegroom.

'Our dresses were of white muslin and Valenciennes lace (made at Marshall & Snelgrove, where I also recall going to be fitted) with sashes of deep yellow, yellow stockings with bronze shoes and bouquets of yellow sweet sultan completed our attire.

'I remember the excitement of the drive to Coltishall Church on that great occasion and walking along the red carpetted pathway amidst an admiring throng of interested spectators. Aunt Margaret, who drove with the two small bridesmaids to the church was actually so indulgent as to allow them to sit on the front seat of the carriage, as befitted the important part they were to take in the proceedings.'

Little Dorothy Lake also spent some time at the seaside, at Mundesley. It was a particular joy when once she travelled alone with her father. They had luncheon on the train as a great treat, and she was also much amused when father pointed out to her from the window of the railway carriage Sloley Church, which struck her as a most peculiar name.

'One great excitement during our visits to Mundesley was the perodical arrival of sailing coal ships. My brother and I would scurry across the fields to the beach to watch the disembarking of the coal and the carting of it, by mules up the gangways to the Ship Inn.

'To us there was something infinitely picturesque and mysterious about the coming of the coal ship. She would be anchored as close to the shore as possible and as the tide went out would remain high and dry on the beach, while the process of unloading her began in full earnest; then towards evening, as the tide crept slowly in again, she would gradually float, lonely and silently, away. My brother always made a collection for the crew and went round with the hat himself to all the occupants of the beach for that purpose.'

Cricket was mostly the prerogative of those who had been educated at the public schools in those days. Dorothy recalls during one of her holidays at Coltishall being taken to a cricket match at Gunton Hall, in which several of her young uncles were playing. It was a long drive which she very much enjoyed.

On another occasion she records 'My young uncles' cricket team gave a dance at the Manor House, when I was about seven or eight. Preparations included the erecting of a large marquee on the lawn for a ballroom, with passageways leading from the house, which thrilled me with keenest interest. Being allowed to hand round dance programmes (the pencils of which were pale pink and pale blue) in an old silver cake basket and to sit up eating ices until well after midnight, made it one of the great occasions of my life.'

Four of her uncles sailed a good deal on the river and Broads and each had his own boat, known as the Four Aces, being called Hearts, Diamonds, Clubs and Spades.

Wherries and Holiday-makers

The opening of the railway signalled the ending of the cargo carrying wherries, but it also brought the county within easy reach of London. Soon holidays afloat began to be fashionable and popular among the wealthy and leisured classes. At first the old wherries were merely adapted for the accommodation of holiday parties during the summer months whilst still being used for trading in the winter. Publicity was given to this lovely unspoilt area by the display of photographs in almost every compartment of passenger trains, and several books were published by intrepid adventurers who set out to explore the wilds of Norfolk.

Wherries were a type of sailing barge peculiar to Norfolk and they immediately caught the imaginations of London visitors. They were shallow draught vessels carrying cargoes of round about 30 tons. The huge mast, weighted at the bottom by one or two tons of lead was stepped well forward and supported an equally huge sail. In spite of their great size both mast and sail could be easily lowered by the crew of two men or one man and a boy, when it was necessary to pass under the many low-arched bridges.

Another characteristic of this type of craft was, to quote the wherrymen, that 'they could sail as close to the wind' as any known craft. That is to say they could sail almost against the wind which was made possible by the mast being situated so far forward.

The colour scheme was almost always the same. The hull above the waterline was black with a white patch symmetrically placed on each side of the bow, generally known at the wherry's 'face'. The hatches which covered the hold and the small living quarters of the crew were usually deep red and were supported about 18 inches above the deck by a series of movable blocks of wood kept in position by irons. The irons were generally black and the woodwork white. The squared section at the foot of the mast was also painted white.

W.A.Dutt in *The Norfolk Broads* published in the early 1900s writes of seeing a wherry 'which had only that morning left a Coltishall wherry-builder's yard, where it had been repainted. It had red, white and blue bands round the top of the mast and beneath them was a two-feet band of burnished brass; flag, tabernacle blocks and cabin roof were vermillion, and the tiller and cabin doors were royal blue and yellow. The wherry was 'light' and showed something of a pale green keel. All these colours reflected in the water, where they shimmered and melted into one another whenever a breath of wind or a passing boat sent ripples running towards the shore.'

The deck itself was very limited, consisting of a narrow way on each side of the hold and extending from the stern to the small space ahead of the

Allen's boatyard, where you could hire a wherry with a crew of two for £12 a week.

mast. On each side on the base of the mast was a plate with the name of the wherry, its owner and the place from which it hailed. The lettering was done with great care, some proud owners even going to the expense of gold leaf. The knowledgeable could identify an approaching wherry long before the name plates could be seen, by the rings of various colours on the part of the mast above the sail. Each owner had his own arrangement of rings.

Sometimes the wind was dead against them, or there was no wind at all - then the wherrymen would keep the craft moving by the use of quants. These were very long poles with an iron shod fork at the bottom and a knob at the top. The men would walk to the bow of the vessel, plunge the fork end of the quant into the water, place the knob against their shoulder and walk along the narrow plankway to the stern, pushing the craft beneath their feet.

This was a laborious task and it required a considerable skill, particularly in the ability to withdraw the quant from the bottom of the muddy river at the end of the walk. The experienced quanter knew just when to begin the withdrawal and also the correct twist to liberate the quant from the mud. Failure to do this correctly might easily result in the quant being left standing in solitary state sticking out of the water many yards behind the wherry or worse still in the quanter finding himself hanging like a monkey on a stick, with the wherry gone from under his feet.

P.H.Emerson in his book *On English Lagoons* writes 'no conversions are more interesting than those of Norfolk wherries. After having led boisterous and irregular lives, many of these strange craft don fresh dresses - become family house-boats and settle down to respectable careers.' His own boat 'one of the prettiest models afloat' was originally named *The Little Spark* and was used to carry marl between the pits at Horstead and the big river wherries. Later she was sold to the Columbia Fishing Fleet and was used to carry ice.

The ice industry has completely disappeared but was then of no little importance. When the dykes and upper reaches of the rivers were frozen over, as they were whenever the weather was at all severe, the wherrymen turned their hands to the loading of ice cargoes. The fishing fleets of Yarmouth and Lowestoft depended upon good supplies of ice and this was stored in ice-houses until it was needed later in the year.

The ice was dydled off the surface of the broads with wire dydles about two feet across set on the ends of lengthy poles, rather similar to the implements used by marshmen for fying out dykes. When a wherry had a full hold of this chilly cargo it would be sailed to one or other of the fishing ports and unloaded at one of the icehouses. Some of the large private houses such as the Manor House at Coltishall had their own ice-house.

'Icing,' wrote Emerson of his treasured pleasure wherry, 'was terribly rough on her skin and did much to spoil her complexion and age her. After that ill-considered venture collapsed, she fell into the hands of one Gaby Thomas. I know not to what base uses she was not put by him - she even carried ash-pit siftings - was once sunk and fished up again and finally Gaby died, but the *Spark* flew onwards, passing through many hands until she fell into the clutches of old Tommy, the one-eyed winkle-seller.

'He too, used her for icing and it was at such work that I saw my beauty and determined to possess her. The one-eyed winkle merchant hummed and hah-ed and sold her for a small sum, his single eye glittering greedily as he signed the receipt and pocketed the money. I quickly gave her over to the dressmakers and in five weeks she was converted. I renamed her *Maid of the Mist*.'

At that time, a trip to the Broads, four hours by train from London, smacked of adventure. Pleasure craft were rapidly being built, wherries converted and there were small steamers available for those who could not sail. In fact it scarcely mattered whether you could manage a boat or not, because the cost of hire usually included the services of a man who acted as sailing-master, cook and steward and a lad for washing-up, potato peeling, fish-cleaning and the like. Many were the men and boys from Coltishall who found work in this way - and a great boon it was too.

A wherry, with crew of two accommodating about a dozen persons could be hired for £12 to £14 per week. But since the average worker earned only 10s to 15s (50p to 75p) it was only those who were at least passing rich, who could afford a Broads holiday.

In the late 1880s Allen's yard was advertising 'Yachts and Boats to let for the Season on most reasonable terms; Gentlemen's Boats taken charge of for the winter in good dry Store Rooms. All classes of boats built. Estimates given.

The *Merlin* Cutter-rigged Yacht; sleeping accommodation for three. Terms £3.10s per week, including man.

The *Bessie* Lug sail open boat, with awning. Terms £1 per week, including man.

The *Florence* Lug Sail open boat, with awning. Terms £1.10 per week.

For gentleman's yachting apparel, white flannels were very much in vogue, with a straw hat or brightly coloured cap. Ladies, it was suggested should don navy serge, made up as plainly as possible to minimise the risk of volumimous skirts becoming entangled among the boughs or the oars. Actually their presence on small boats was felt to be somewhat out of place altogether, as there was insufficient privacy for them and the voyage called for a certain amount of hardiness.

A few Wherry Yachts however were advertised as being suitable for the fairer sex, among them the *Bertha, Kate* and *Diligent*. These had been specially fitted with a Ladies' Cabin which included washstand, looking glass and lockers. The gentlemen's cabin, twice as long, would sleep four or six gentlemen but doubled in the daytime for a dining-saloon and was fitted with a table down the centre and sitting space for eight or ten. The cabins throughout were furnished with blinds, soft cushions, plenty of rugs and were lighted at night by lamps; They were divided by a gangway leading from the deck. The w.c. could be entered from either the fore or aft cabins and was 'private to each'. Two men were provided by the owners to look after and sail the yachts as well as attending to the cooking, cleaning and washing-up and to the wants of the party on board.

Seats were provided on the foredeck of the yacht and a 'jolly boat' accompanied each. They were provided with all necessary glass, crockery, cutlery and table linen, and the men's cabin was fitted with a good cooking stove. A piano could be provided. How delightful for your day's sailing to end with a Victorian musical evening, there in the wherry, by the reeded banks of the moonlit waters - in fact in much the same location as any modern holidaymaker might chose.

Looking back on his childhood in Anchor Street, Billy Allen remarked how much manual labour went into boat building in those days. The only forms of machine used were the cumbersome and powerful jacks, two or three of which could move a wherry on land into a convenient position. There was also the windlass with pulleys and ropes which was used to haul wherries ashore for repairs, recaulking and re-pitching their hulls.

Through the head of the windlass two long poles were thrust and at each end a man would push in the same clockwise direction, gradually winding the rope round the windlass, drawing up the wherry inch by inch until it was quite out of the water. Billy Allen recalled 'We boys of Anchor Street loved to add our little to the push and in spite of the fact that some could barely reach the poles, imagined we were helping, the men good-naturedly allowing us.'

One event which took place only once or twice a year and which aroused more excitement than any other, was the launching of a wherry, especially if it was a new one. For days before the boys would be full of hopes that it would not take place during school hours. Occasionally the children were placed aboard the craft before she was gently lowered by jacks on to the slipway. One by one the supporting props were removed and the wherry began to move, at first slowly, but increasing slightly in speed until she entered the water with a splash.

Of another occasion Billy Allen wrote - 'One day we boys were watching the men drawing boiling pitch from a cauldron when every now and then they drew what looked like a solid lump of pitch. Much to our surprise we were told they were potatoes. By the time they were cool enough to handle they were covered by a layer of solid pitch. A sharp knife soon removed this unnatural skin revealing a beautiful white, floury potato free from any skin or any taint of pitch. With a pinch of salt the men began to eat them and invited us to taste the repast. I have often related this incident to people outside the village and have never met anyone who had ever heard of potatoes cooked in this way and I am afraid some of them seemed to think I had peculiar taste.'

As Others Saw Us

 Ernest R.Suffling in *Land of the Broads* looked hard at the natives of Norfolk and wrote 'The type of their features is certainly Danish - straight noses, open frank countenances, blue or grey eyes, fair skin, ruddy complexion and straw-coloured hair.' His description could well be applied to many of the truly local residents of the village today.

On language he wrote it 'is interspersed with semi-Danish words and the accent and pronunciation are, by reason of their Danish extraction, unlike those of any other English dialect. Most of the Danish sea-kings and their followers had particular cognomens, by which they were known irrespective of their family names, such as 'Sea-wolf', 'Foam-borne', 'The 'Dragon', and this custom has been handed down to the present generation, as nearly every man has a *sobriquet* or nickname.

Most of these names were given to their recipients when boys, but were retained to the grave. When they went into employment these nicknames took the place of their baptismal names and by them, and frequently by them alone, they were known. He does add 'the martial or sublime of the Danish names has however descended to the ridiculous' which can certainly be illustrated by a few of the nicknames from Coltishall 'Blucher', 'Tich' 'Doughy' or 'Shiner'.

'The dress of the natives' also caught the attention of Ernest Suffling. 'The long-sleeved waistcoat is worn by most of them. It is of somewhat peculiar make, being very long in the body, so as to come well over the hips. The front is of velveteen, with plenty of buttons and the back and sleeves are of jean. The turnover of the cuffs is also of velveteen when the wearer is at all a beau.

'The long smock, with its elaborate breastwork, so well known in many parts of England, is almost absent here but its place is taken by the slop, which is made exactly like the French blouse, but is white or nearly so in colour. It is a simple square-cut garment, with a hole in the top for the head to come through and baggy sleeves, fastened at the wrist with a button. This is a very sensible garment for fieldwork. Buskins are usually worn in wet weather and stout hobnailed boots encase the feet.

'The head has a hat of flexible felt, which may be worn in a number of ways, according to the fancy of the owner. Sometimes the hat is worn *a la* brigand, with one side of the brim curled up and the front thrust out, like a peak *a la* Mephistopheles; and in many other ways. In wet weather it is turned down all round and looks like the roof-thatch on a round stack, but answers its purpose admirably as a shelter from the rain. It is a hat for all weathers. Contrast it with the fine-weather, glossy silk hat of the town man, the supposed mark of respectability and I am afraid for utility and comfort, the latter will only be second.

Coltishall Lock. Visitors were advised to take the train from Coltishall to Aylsham rather than pass through the never-ending locks and bridges.

'There is one peculiar article of dress that may be noted - the Sunday collar, if you please, as during the week a coloured handkerchief, wound round the neck like a rope, takes its place. It is fastened by a button in front, then passed *backwards* round the neck, the strings again brought to the front and tied. Should a button fastening an ordinary collar come off, a man (a town man) is helpless; but in this one, if a string gives way a piece of twine, or part of a boot lace is spliced on and all is well again.'

Londoners were advised to stock up with provisions before venturing into the remoteness of Norfolk, though of course, there were plentiful supplies to be had at the bigger towns and villages, like Coltishall. Ernest Suffling advised - 'Bread can usually be procured at the villages on the route, say, every second day; but as at times it is not procurable, a supply of biscuits should be taken.

'As these trips are mostly taken during the summer months, tinned food is consumed to a large extent, as fresh meat and other perishable articles soon become tainted in the confined and hot lockers. It may be well to point out that a good supply of ice may be procured at Yarmouth from the ice-house on the quay.

'The supply of fresh meat cannot be relied upon, as few of the villages can boast of a butcher's shop and in those that do, no animal is killed until enough orders have been given to ensure the sale of the whole carcase.'

Visitors to Wroxham had to sail on to Coltishall, to find a butcher or a baker. There was also a baker at Salhouse, but there they only baked once a week. Norfolk was said to be noted for bad cheese. Only the strongest tobacco was stocked in the village shops and decent cigars were unobtainable. Spirits were said to be of the fiery, untamed order and Norfolk beer villainous and undrinkable. Water for cooking was usually taken from the river, but drinking water was procured from the cottage wells, unless, as often happened, the cottager used the river water for drinking anyway.

Not the least of the joys of such a holiday would be the sight of windmills merrily turning - though even at that time, much of their work was being taken over by steam-pumps. Above all, the waterways would never be crowded. One could voyage up the Bure as far as Aylsham, though Suffling advised visitors to take the train to Aylsham from Coltishall rather than pass through the never-ending locks and bridges. Wherrymen were so expert in handling their craft that this was less of a hazard for them.

G.C.Davies in *Norfolk Broads and Rivers* included this fascinating description - 'On you go before a strong breeze until within a hundred yards of the bridge, when the sail is sheeted flat; the man goes leisurely forward, leaving his wife or son at the helm, lets the windlass run; down comes the sail; the gaff has then to be detached from the mast and laid on top of the hatches; then, just as you think the mast must crash against the bridge, it falls gently back and you shoot under; up it goes again without a pause, the forestay is made fast and under the pressure of the windlass the heavy sail rises aloft, all before you have quite got over your first impulse of alarm.'

The River in Winter

 One who did make the trip to Aylsham and back by river was Emerson - and he chose to do it in winter. 'Our (return) journey down to Coltishall was one triumphant procession through a gallery of exquisite landscapes such as no painter ever caught on canvas, but alas! they were so evanescent that on the morrow they would have disappeared.' On 23rd February 1891 they moored by Colishall bridge and 'a sleepy fly came out of his hiding-place.'

'Our first morning at Coltishall revealed another rime-frosted landscape. The wintry breath had decorated the dead umbelliferae on the banks with exquisite silver frostings. Nature seemed to have preserved these dead stalks as skeleton frames for her ornamental work, so delightfully did she blend her silver crystals on the ebony stems; but alas, the sun soon destroyed her handiwork. The pure frosted stage, when the dead stalks were all white with snowy powder, lasting only till the sun was strong enough to melt some of the crystals. At this stage, the work is the most beautiful; but as the crystals melt all their sharp outlines disappear, their purity of colour is lost, the mass becomes greyish and formless.

'In the evening the Salvation Army Band came jarring through the mist. We followed it to discover the hardiness of these Christians upon such a night. This was as we expected - but a handful of devotees followed the music. Even the guinea fowls calling to the misty moon were more zealous than they.

'As we followed them up a street two girls stood giggling at the door.

' "There go Mr Jones," said one.

' "Oh, I ha' seen you, Mr Jones" they shouted and ran indoors.

'I found out afterwards that Mr Jones was a respected native. In the mist they had mistaken me for him, surmising, perhaps that I was on the spree, and thus easily originated a scandal.

'As we reached the higher parts of Coltishall the mists disappeared, but as the band of devotees did not increase, we retraced our steps, returning through the mist to our ship, round which the air seemed filled with the sounds of lovers. Low whistles and suppressed laughter greeted us on all sides. Coltishall is evidently an amorous town.

'As we stepped aboard, a great rat dived into the river and we stood silently in the mist listening to two girls tormenting some poor fellow in a garden across the water. I shouted through the mist, the bridge echoed, and they fled with shouts of laughter, deserting the poor wight, whom we heard crashing like a mad bull through the hedge. A man with a lantern came down to his cucumber house and made up the fires, for a rime frost already covered the ground.'

The next morning 'six degrees of frost proved that the gardener was wise in looking after his cucumbers. After breakfast, old Bob turned up and we went into his little wooden house, where we drank a good bottle of old ale and smoked a first-rate cigar.'

Old Bob was 'a sterling good-hearted man who, though he had met with many reverses, has with rare wisdom learnt therefrom how to live. Once he kept a pack of hounds, for a keener sportsman never breathed, but bad times came and Old Bob buckled to and went into business, starting housekeeping in a snug little wooden home where he had learnt that true happiness is to be found within doors and not in a showy exterior. Such a good fellow is he that the "little shanty", as his friends call the hut, is always full of laughter and jollity. Old Bob is the philosopher of Coltishall, where he lives a bachelor life with his sister, a real good-hearted woman, who keeps his house and helps in the business.

'On our return to the boat, we passed several beech hedges covered with old leaves, warm and picturesque in colour and form; they make most suitable hedges for gardens. On the way home Old Bob told us that in the old times they used to breed hares for sporting purposes. They mixed the breed with hares procured from other districts, marking the offspring before they turned them off. They found these mongrels ran faster, and gave better sport.

' "But hunting is going out here," said Bob regretfully. "No one had any money to subscribe to the packs or keep hunters - the country is getting very dull!" '

On Friday, 27th February 1891, Emerson and his party left Coltishall. 'As we sailed through the thin ice lining the river banks, numerous birds were busy getting their breakfast. There were kingfishers, coal-tits, chaffinches, starlings, waterhens, woodpigeons, rooks and a hoody. The river was full of roach. A garden on the bank was bright with snowdrops bearing a fanciful resemblance to veiled communicants going through the fields.'

They followed the winding river, passing the tree-fringed stream below the lock where they startled a waterhen feeding on the bank, and starlings and tomtits from the tree tops.

'Soon Coltishall, with its richly-coloured malthouses and picturesque residences was left behind. The sun arose at noon, the thermometer rising to 70 degrees, so that we lit no fire in the cabin. There was a nice little south-easterly breeze and we sailed joyfully through the winding river, passing cottage girls beating carpets in the warm sunshine and gardeners busy digging their beds. Below Coltishall some men were felling elm trees on a patch of marshland.

At half past eleven Belaugh Church hove in sight, but so much does the river wind here that we did not lose sight of its square tower till 2.30 except on one occasion for a few minutes. In a garden at Belaugh we saw a white butterfly flitting through a hedgerow and it is worthy of remark that exactly opposite was a dyke covered with ice. As we sailed along we flushed out several pairs of partridges and mallard.'

Our River

The river played a major part in the summer activities of the people of Coltishall, and it was always simply called 'our river'. The name Bure was not included in the list of English rivers learned at school and many villagers never knew it.

Towards the end of the last century an attempt was made to hold an annual regatta, which was supported by the boat-builders. The programme included races for sailing craft and rowing boats with some swimming to give variety. The committee barge was moored by the bank of the river near the boatyards and the sailing races started there, proceeded upstream to a buoy opposite the Hall, turned downstream to another buoy near the boundary with Belaugh, then back to the starting point. The regattas failed after two or three years however because the entries were so small.

During the summer months a steam boat ran once a week bringing parties of trippers from Wroxham to the Anchor Staithe. Rowing boats could be hired from the White Horse and those who could afford it enjoyed peaceful sailing. There was always fishing for the men and boys and families enjoyed a river picnic on a fine summer day.

Coltishall bridge after the Great Flood of 1912.

Many of the children and young men preferred to be in the river rather than on it and the most popular swimming place was alongside the towpath, just beyond the 'little black bridge' opposite Horstead common. In fine weather they would be there every day and all day if they got the chance. The river had a good bottom, especially after Mr Patteson moved into Hautbois House and had gravel put down. He also built a couple of corrugated iron changing rooms. Dredging spoiled it but in those days it was a fine bathing place, and there was the challenge of having a good long swim - sometimes as far as the bridge, or even the lock and back. A young man could stand anywhere in the river unless there was a really high tide.·

Willie Wilson recalls 'In summer we often went swimming straight from school, just took off our clothes and went in. The Horstead boys would carry their clothes over the river on their heads, then get dressed and go home that way. Men went swimming there too. I remember little Mr Page, the tailor, especially well, because he could do a somersault when he dived into the river. I never remember the girls swimming there, but they tell me that they did.'

Seasonal Customs

 The new year was always announced by full peals from the church bells. Already some people were gathered inside to welcome in the New Year with prayer. Most families sat up till after midnight to drink a toast and in some cases arrangements were made for a dark-haired person to be the first to enter the house to ensure a Happy New Year.

When most New Year resolutions had already been forgotten came February 14th, St Valentine's Day. The evening of that day was awaited with great excitement, especially by the children for then, after dark, mysterious presents from unknown donors would be left on the doorstep. On that evening young Billy Allen was allowed to break the normally strict rule of going to bed at seven o'clock, so that he might answer knocks at the door.

At the first knock he would rush to the door and fling it open - no-one was to be seen. Generally, but not always, there was a parcel and he would pick it up, tear it open to see what it contained and then spend ages trying to guess who had left it for him. One such present he recalled which he particularly appreciated and kept for years, until he was an old man, though it was in a dilapidated condition. It was years later that he learned from whom it came, for the trick was to be as secret as possible in the giving.

Not always was there such a pleasant surprise, for sometimes just as the child stooped to pick up the parcel, it would suddenly jump away. Some practical joker had attached a long string to what appeared to be a present and under cover of darkness snatched it away and before he could be discovered had disappeared.

Little Dorothy Lake, then back home in London, also recalled the thrill of St Valentine's Day. 'For several years while we were small, my mother made February 14th an excuse for the game of Valentines and the particular manner in which these little gifts were distributed added greatly to our enjoyment.

'How well I remember, during the "children's hour", in the drawing-room after tea, that sudden and mysterious "rat-tat-tat" which sent us flying to open the door, to discover lying just outside on the mat, a parcel addressed to either my brother or myself. The first "rat-tat" would be followed, at intervals of about five or ten minutes, by further rappings and further discoveries of perhaps two or more parcels for each of us.

'The lightning disappearance of the person who had placed the parcels thus, added considerable zest and made us wonder whether St Valentine himself had a hand in the game, though in later years I had a suspicion that a certain recess on the landing might have been a convenient hiding place and that it was perhaps Bird, our parlourmaid, or Ackie, our Nannie.'

Whit Monday Fair

An entry in the school log-book demonstrates the importance of the annual Whit Monday Fair and the disruption it caused at the end of the last century. 'May 10th, 1875. Whit-Monday - Coltishall Fair - only 70 children present (out of a roll of 126) 32 hold up their hands as expecting to come in the afternoon. It is probable there will not be more than a dozen. A half-holiday is therefore deemed advisable.'

A week later on 17th May 'Only 72 present in the morning and 65 in the afternoon - the revel at the fair is still raging and likely to be kept up for some days.' The unfortunate schoolmaster, whose pay depended upon the numbers of children actually attending, added a plaintive query - 'Would it not have been better if the Board, knowing the festive customs of the place, had given a week's holiday rather than have reduced the yearly average by keeping the school open?'

His plea was evidently listened to, for the following year the entry for June 2nd reads - 'The school breaks up today for a week's holiday at Whitsuntide.' One can almost hear the master's sigh of relief as he dipped his pen in the ink to write those words.

As far as the children were concerned the fair was one of the highlights of the year. It was set up on the top common. 'Stocks Fair that was a good one!' declared Ralph Wells. 'They come over the bridge with the traction engine pulling the bit wagons and when they was all set up then they'd use that to make the music and turn the rides. Rhubarb Underwood, he used to bring his fair sometimes, but he never had many sideshows and he just travelled with horses, not with a traction engine. People used to come from miles around - from Sco Ruston and Tunstead, especially the young men and sometimes there used to be fights.

'I really liked the fair. My father, he'd be playing bowls in the evening on the White Horse bowling green and he'd buy me a bottle of ginger beer and some hollow biscuits. They were made by Coopers of Norwich and they sold them at the fair. Lovely big biscuits they were, not sweet, but really good. I used to think they were a great treat. The ones from the fair were bigger than the ones we used to make at the bakery where I worked later.

'It was at the Whit Monday Fair that I first saw a moving picture. A biograph they called it - more like a magic lantern. I was only a schoolboy and I remember going there along with my father. It was in a big tent, on the fairground. The film was about poachers - a policeman was chasing these poachers and one of the poachers, he turned round and shot the policeman. Then there was a real chase until the poachers were caught. I really enjoyed that - I was absolutely thrilled! I've never forgotten it!

The Oddfellows

The annual parade of the Oddfellows, known as the Loyal William Fox Lodge, which was opened in 1847, was a big occasion. Most wage earning men were members and many entered their sons under fourteen into a junior branch. For a subscription of 6d a week they could ensure free medical attention for themselves and their wives. Moreover if they were unable to work they could draw 10/- a week (50p), which was always alluded to as being 'on the club'. If and when they reached the age of 70 they drew an annuity of 1/3d (7p) a week - before then there was only the workhouse.

The Oddfellows had a pretty strict medical check before they would admit any young man to their membership. Willie Wilson wanted to join when he was sixteen, but was unable to, because by then the war had started and they reckoned he would be a pretty bad risk; when he was demobilised he was a physical wreck, unable to work for a year and then they thought he was an even worse risk! It was not until 1937 that he eventually joined.

The Lodge organised fetes to raise money, an annual dinner for members and a church parade once a year, but the biggest event on their calendar was the Gala Day. Then members assembled on the top common and were joined by representatives from the Lodges of neighbouring villages, each lining up behind its own brightly coloured banner and the officials wearing their insignia of office. Stirringly led by a band either from the Salvation Army or from the Wesleyan Chapel, they marched along the street, past the church and on towards Coltishall Hall. More and more people joined to follow in their wake. Money was collected from those who lined the route and, so that none should escape, men carried bags on long poles to hold up to those who watched from bedroom windows.

The Hall gardens, carefully tended by full-time gardeners, were always worth a visit, and there was the added attraction of bowls on the private green and the winner received a valued prize. There were also stalls supplying light refreshment, home grown vegetables and flowers, eggs, home-baked cakes and items of needlework, knitting and crochet, painstakingly produced by diligent housewives.

Leisure

In common with most villages at that time, there was little to occupy leisure hours, short as they were. There were no cinemas or bingo halls and the nearest theatre or music hall was in Norwich, but as the last train to Coltishall left when the production was still in full swing, it was impossible for most villagers to attend.

There was not even a village hall. The Church Room was not built until 1910 so there was nowhere for entertainments to be staged. The only place available for such meetings was the school, but evening use of it was frowned upon by the management, except upon an occasion such as the School Prize distribution. This was accompanied by an entertainment given by the pupils to which parents and friends were invited. It usually consisted of singing by classes of children, recitations by the star pupils and ended with a scene from one of Shakespeare's plays.

Wrights – the first garage in the village was beside the bakery. It was also a cycle shop. The picture is dated about 1906. (Photo: Billy Stibbons)

There were, of course, the nine pubs, in which men, sometimes with their wives, could gather for a gossip with friends over a drink. Beer was cheap and in contrast to the opinion of the rich Londoners on the pleasure boats, local opinion pronounced it 'good stuff in them days!'

Ralph Wells said 'The beer was so good, if you had a couple of pints of mild, you started to talk. There were one or two who used to get drunk regular. I remember one old bloke, he had a little white pony and cart, and he sometimes came out of the pub so drunk, he didn't know where he was going, but that pony knew. He'd take the old boy home all right.

'His wife used to square him up sometimes. Then you'd see the old boy with a bit of plaster on his face where she'd hit him. He used to get down to the King's Head and his old woman, she'd come after him. Then the other blokes that were in the bar, they'd persuade the old gal to have a drink and then another and another, till in the end she'd be as drunk as her old man was!

'This old bloke, he used to do a lot of fishing too. He used to boast - not about the size of the fish he caught, but about his money.

' "I've got plenty of money in the bank,' he used to say.

' "Yes in the river bank!" they used to tease him.

'I don't reckon he had much really - couldn't have had, he'd a-drunk it all away.'

Allen's Stores and the King's Head. 'The beer was so good, if you had a couple of pints of mild, you started to talk!'

Towards the End of the Year

In the eighteenth century it was the custom when harvest had ended for the labourers to visit neighbouring farmers from whom they would receive a gift of money. Mary Hardy refers to this in her diary as 'largesse' - though her spelling varies. For example, on Tuesday 13th September 1774 'Mr Lubbock's men here for larges' and again 'S.Nash's men here for larges, Mr Fitt's men ditto for larges of hobis; Mr Broom's men ditto of Horstead, Mr Mack's ditto of Tunstead'. Indeed it sounds quite an expensive time for the farmer. On Saturday 17th September she writes 'The men gathering largesse all day, had their frollick at the Sergeant this evening.' Mr Hardy came back from business in Norwich at 10 p.m. and then joined his men at their frollick. This custom persisted throughout the nineteenth century.

More recently, on the first Saturday after the harvest had all been gathered in, it was customary for the farmworkers and their families to make a trip to Norwich, for shopping and for pleasure. The extra money earned during the harvest was spent on necessary additions to the clothing of the family and these things were expected to last at least until after the next harvest.

Preparations for Christmas began weeks before December 25th with the making of a rich plum pudding. All the raisins, dates and prunes had to be stoned, a sticky job made easier by dipping fruit and fingers in a bowl of warm water. Children loved to help with this and certainly they delighted in stirring the stiff mixture and making a wish to ensure a Merry Christmas.

In some poorer families, where there might not be quite enough to go round, the Christmas dinner was started with a good helping of batter pudding and gravy, so that the edge was taken off the appetite before tucking into the bird - turkey, goose, duck or chicken or a joint of 'butcher's meat'.

Billy Allen says 'The whole family took part in buying and despatching Christmas greeting cards just before the day, in order that they should be delivered actually on Christmas Day.' Nobody seemed to think that the postmen might like to spend the day at home with their own families, but probably the tips and 'nips' they received made up for this inconvenience.

In Billy Allen's home the holly was chosen for a Christmas tree and before hanging trinkets on it, many of the leaves were daubed with melted butter and granulated white sugar sprinkled on them to give the effect of frost. It was not until he was seventeen years old, and was invited to a party in Norwich that he found to his surprise that the Christmas tree was usually a spruce.

So the seasons come and go and much water has flowed beneath Coltishall bridge since those days. Over all the intervening years the gardens and allotments have been dug each autumn and sown in the spring, the Salvation Army Band has paraded playing its familiar hymns, the fortunes of the football and cricket teams have fluctuated to the joy or sorrow of their supporters, and a variety of clubs and societies have been formed to keep the community spirit alive.

In the late 1980s the village still thrives. Hundreds of holiday-makers sail up from Wroxham on their cruisers, and thousands of people come by car to enjoy the river scene from the lower common. The view across the Bure, over the water meadows, to the woods at Heggatt is as lovely as ever. Coltishall still has a cachet as a pleasant place in which to live - Mr Suffling would be hard pressed to differentiate between its inhabitants and those of the Metropolis! The importance of the river to its economy may be less obviously commercial, but undoubtedly it is still considerable - though it is very seldom nowadays that a wherry sails by.

HOTEL NORWICH,
BOUNDARY ROAD,
NORWICH, NORFOLK.